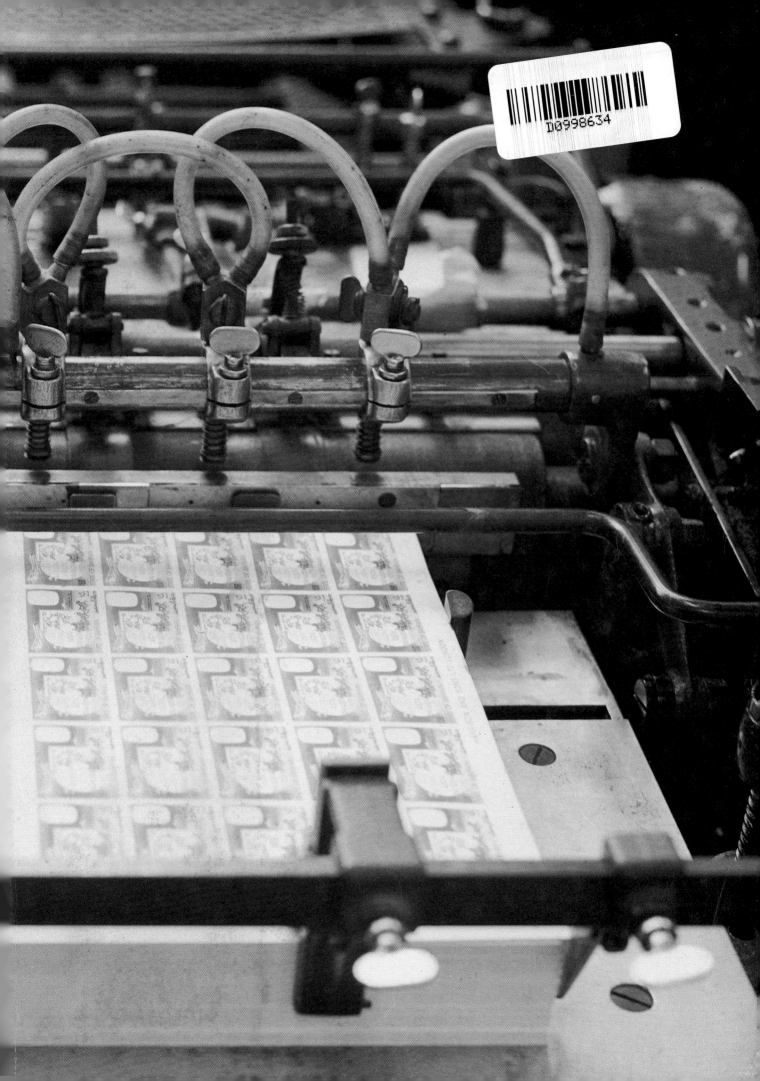

# All color book of
# *Stamps*

## Kenneth Chapman & Barbara Baker

# Contents

4    *The First Stamps*

10  *The Envelope Tells the Story*

18  *Postal History on Stamps*

22  *Commemorative Stamps*

34  *Thematic Collecting*

48  *Stamps Used for Propaganda*

54  *Designing Stamps*

62  *Something Went Wrong*

66  *They look Good–but...*

72  *Acknowledgments*

# The First Stamps

The world's first adhesive postage stamps were the world-famous Penny Black and Twopence Blue issued in Great Britain on 1 May 1840, and valid for public use from 6 May onwards. Before that, all letters had to be handed in over the post office counter where the postage was assessed; it varied according to the distance the letter was to travel and the number of sheets of paper on which it was written (envelopes were virtually unknown, letters being folded and sealed by wax).

Rowland Hill, a one-time schoolmaster, urged reform of the postal system from 1837 onwards and his scheme was finally adopted in 1839 and put into effect in 1840. His reforms established a new principle: that letters could travel anywhere within the United Kingdom for a basic charge of one penny up to $\frac{1}{2}$oz weight; two pence up to 1oz and higher rates for heavier letters. All the time-consuming record keeping and accountancy required by the old system was abolished at a stroke.

The British system was first copied by the Swiss Canton of Zurich, which issued 4 rappen and 6 rappen stamps in March 1843, and then by Brazil which followed suit in August 1843 with 30 reis, 60 reis and 90 reis stamps.

America's first issue was in New York in July 1845. A beautifully engraved portrait of George Washington, as used on the then current bank note of the United States Government, graced a 5 cent stamp inscribed 'Post Office' at the top. Although intended for use within the state of New York only, this stamp was used experimentally in other major cities in the east and was followed in July 1847 by 5 cent and 10 cent stamps issued by the United States Government for general use throughout the country.

The first British colonial territory to use an adhesive stamp was the island of Trinidad where a 5 cent stamp was issued on 24 April 1847 by David Brice, owner of the steamer S.S. *Lady McCleod* which plied along the coast from Port of Spain to San Fernando, carrying letters either way for merchants in the two towns. The stamp bore no indication of face value but carried in the upper half a picture of the *Lady McCleod*. It thus claims a double 'first', since apart from being the British Empire's first adhesive, it was the first pictorial stamp, the design having something other than a royal portrait or just figures of values.

The postal validity of all these stamps was limited, Britain's to within the confines of the United Kingdom, Zurich's to within the Canton, Brazil's to her territory and the *Lady McCleod* stamps to letters the ship carried. When the General Postal Union (now the Universal Postal Union) was set up in 1874, international validity was accorded to the stamps of member nations.

Mauritius, a tiny British colony in the Indian Ocean, was the next on the scene, with the first stamps to bear the name of the place of origin. Its two so-called 'Post Office' stamps, issued on 21 September 1847, have held a premier position in the rarity and value tables of the philatelic world ever since.

Only 500 of each were printed and less than 40 of the 1,000 stamps are known today. The printer was commissioned to base his design on the Penny Black but to engrave the words 'Post Paid' along the left-hand side of the stamp and Mauritius along the right-hand side. In error, he engraved 'Post Office'.

When France joined the select band of stamp-issuing countries on 1 January 1849, her first issue was inscribed Repub. Franc. by way of identification. Neighbouring Belgium took the plunge on 1 July 1849 with two stamps featuring King Leopold I but without any other indication of national origin.

Bavaria, as an independent German kingdom, took advantage of the new system and issued 1 kreutzer, 3 kreutzer and 6 kreutzer stamps inscribed 'Bayern' in 1849. They were only notable for being in a square format, unlike the rectangular format of all earlier issues.

The first decade of the history of adhesive postage stamps closed on this sombre note, hardly relieved by the appearance of Spain's first stamps on 1 January 1850 bearing a somewhat crudely engraved portrait of Queen Isabella II. The first Austrian stamp, which followed exactly six months later, introduced a new theme for stamp design, the country's coat of arms. These stamps, undistinguished in design, are a constant source of interest to specialist collectors because their numerous printings over the eight years of their currency can be identified and classified.

The kingdom of Saxony issued a single 3 pfennig value in June 1850, merely inscribed 'Sachsen'. Two other German countries joined the club that year: the kingdom of Prussia whose first stamps featured King Frederick William IV and were valued in pfennig and silbergroschen; and two unusual stamps authorized by the local authorities in Schleswig-Holstein with their arms embossed in white relief in the central vignette. The currency was in schillings and the indication of origin simply S and H in the upper corners.

A selection of early issues including *Great Britain's* 1d black and 2d blue of 1840, the world's first adhesive postage stamps. Neither of these is rare in used condition, the value of an average to good 1d black being £10 ($25) and the 2d blue about two and one half times that. Unused they are much more valuable, about £100 ($250) and £200 ($500) respectively. Other stamps above include the very rare 1847 2d blue Post Office issue of *Mauritius*, the 1851 12d black of *Canada*, three Italian States stamps – *Naples* (1858), *Tuscany* (1851) and *Sicily* (1859). *Victoria* (Australia) is represented by the locally produced 'half-length' issue of 1850. *Van Diemens Land* (now Tasmania) and *New Zealand* both made use of the

Chalon portrait head (see page 55) of Queen Victoria on their stamps of 1855. *New South Wales* first used, in 1850, stamps known as 'Sydney Views' from the rough engraving of Sydney which is the central feature of the design. The ever-popular *Cape of Good Hope* triangulars, first issued in 1853, were deliberately shaped this way so that the stamps would be distinctive and letters bearing them be easily sorted from letters with the then orthodox rectangular stamps. Canada's first issue (1851) also adopted the Chalon portrait for the top value, the 12d in black, a colour which resulted in one of the finest Chalon Head stamps ever printed. The stamp is a popular variety and sells for £1,000

($2,500) upwards according to its condition. The 1s purple from *Nova Scotia* (1851) and the 1s vermilion stamp from *Newfoundland* (1857) were among the earliest to incorporate a floral design.

All these early stamps shared a common feature: they were printed by the same process, which is known to collectors as line engraving and to most printers as the direct-plate process. The reason was security. It was thought that the highly individual and skilled work of engraving a printing die by hand was sufficiently difficult to deter anyone from attempting to produce forgeries.

[Left] The first three stamps issued in *America*. [Left] The 5¢ *New York* Postmaster stamp of 1845; picturing George Washington it was issued by the Postmaster for use in New York (named in the upper corners of the stamp), but was used in other towns including Washington D.C. [Centre and right] The first national stamps were the 5¢ Benjamin Franklin and the 10¢ George Washington of 1847. They replaced all the Postmaster stamps throughout the country on 1 July 1847, but exactly four years later became the only government-issued United States stamps ever to be invalidated. All issues from 1851 may still be used.

[Right] Late starters among stamp-issuing countries were the Baltic States of *Estonia*, *Latvia* and *Lithuania* who, following World War I, seized their long-awaited independence from Russia. Very crude emergency stamps first appeared in 1918, and by 1919 all three states had established their own postal services with definitive stamps. Early in 1940 Russian forces again occupied all three countries to ensure that there was no dissident uprising and to provide a bulwark against German invasion from the West. The three states became unwilling constituent republics of the U.S.S.R. and were once again forced to use Russian stamps. The stamps of these three countries are typical of many states which have achieved independence from a great power and have then been subjugated again by their former masters or have been absorbed into another neighbouring monolithic state. While the first issues of countries such as these three Baltic States are generally hurriedly prepared to ensure the fastest possible external recognition of their hard-won independence, it is noticeable that as they settle down the stamps they issue reflect by their designs individual histories and cultures which, over the centuries, stimulated the urge for freedom from an overbearing foreign power. It is this national approach to stamp designing which makes such a strong appeal to collectors who feel that they acquire a better understanding of the peoples of these countries simply by studying carefully the stories behind the stamp designs issued by them.

Not all first issues go back to the 19th century. The island of *Pitcairn* relied mainly on New Zealand stamps until it acquired Crown Colony status in 1940 and issued its first definitive stamps, the 4d value picturing the Bible taken from H.M.S. *Bounty* when the mutineers landed and settled on Pitcairn. The first stamp of *Salvador* in Central America appeared in 1867 featuring a volcano and seven stars, one for each department of the country. In 1963 the islands forming a dependency of the Falkland Islands were given Crown Colony status, along with some of the Antarctic mainland, as the *British Antarctic Territory*, and issued their own stamps. These give a vivid impression of life at 'the bottom of the world'. *India*'s first general issue was in 1854 and included the 4 annas bi-coloured stamps. For some printings, the impressions on the printing plate were so widely spaced that each single stamp was framed in blue. Most people using the stamps cut away all the margins leaving an octagonal-shaped stamp, now far less valuable than a full-margined copy.

[Right] Here are first issues from three areas: *Malta* (a late printing in a deeper colour than the first); *Liechtenstein's* first stamps (1912) were modelled on the contemporary Austrian issues which were in use there until the principality achieved postal independence; and the *British Virgin Islands*, the Caribbean group which still clings to its colonial status. The figure on the stamp is St Ursula, providing a change from Queen Victoria's portrait. *Ceylon* used the Queen's portrait from the beginning in 1857, and put the 4d rose and 8d brown (illustrated) in an unusually ornate frame. In 1957 *Australia* provided special stamps for its scattered outposts in the Antarctic, the first to be issued being a 2s blue recalling the 1954 expedition which led to the creation of the Australian Antarctic Territory. Subsequent issues by the territory illustrate the meteorological, geographical and marine biology work carried out under conditions of extreme hardship by teams of scientists.

[Above] Three of the 'square' stamps from the former German states of *Baden* (1851), *Bavaria* (1849) and *Saxony* (1850). *Western Australia's* first stamps, in 1854, all feature the indigenous black swan, who only appeared in black on the 1d black. The 1s value of the same issue was the first to employ a transverse oval design. *Katanga* enjoyed a brief existence as a state separate from Congo Kinshasa, formerly the Belgian Congo. The 10¢ is one of the provisional issue of 1960 created by overprinting on obsolete Belgian Congo stamps. The *Etat du Katanga* 1fr 50 stamp is from the first definitive issue of 1961. Within two years Katanga rejoined what then became the Democratic Republic of the Congo which, in 1973, finally adopted the name of Zaïre. *Barbuda*, a dependency of the British colony of Antigua, issued its own stamps briefly in 1922 by overprinting the general issue for the Leeward Islands group of which Antigua was a part. Again from 1968 to 1971 *Barbuda* issued its own stamps under the authority of Antigua which by then had become a 'state in association with Great Britain' and, for the third time, recommenced separate issues in November 1973 on the occasion of the marriage of Princess Anne and Captain Mark Phillips. The *New Brunswick* 5¢ stamp of 1860 was quickly withdrawn because it pictured the colony's Postmaster-General, the Hon. Charles Connell, who had ordered the stamps and refused to withdraw them. He was forced to resign and the stamp was replaced by one with the more orthodox portrait of Queen Victoria.

[Left] A selection of first issues ranging from 1861 to 1941. The first Greek stamps (1851) were modelled on those of France (where they were printed), but portrayed the Greek God Hermes. From 1922 until 1968, the *Republic of Ireland* used definitive stamps which remained unchanged in design, and included 1d, 1½d and 2d stamps showing a map of the whole country, including Northern Ireland which is still a political part of the United Kingdom. Other first issues here are from *Haiti* (1881), *Ethiopia* (1894) and *Labuan* (1879), which eventually became absorbed into the colony of North Borneo (now Sabah and one of the states forming the present Malaysia), and from *Guernsey* which was obliged to issue its own stamps when supplies of British stamps were exhausted during the German wartime occupation. Both Guernsey and Jersey became postally independent of Great Britain in 1969 and now control their own stamp-issuing programmes.

[Right] A unique constitutional arrangement placed the islands of the New Hebrides in the Pacific Ocean under the dual control of Great Britain and France. The first stamps were those of *Fiji* overprinted *New Hebrides*, and of the French colony of *New Caledonia* overprinted *Nouvelles Hebrides*. Both issues appeared in 1908. *Germany's* first stamps following World War II were issued jointly by the British and American occupying forces in 1945: A.M. POST means Allied Military Post. *Nepal*, the ancient and tiny Himalayan kingdom, first issued stamps in 1881 and they remained valid only in Nepal until the country joined the Universal Postal Union in 1959. It has become customary since then to issue a special stamp each year for the king's birthday. The British colonies of *St Vincent* (1861) and *Jamaica* (1880) chose engraved and letter-press portraits of Queen Victoria for their first issues.

[Above] *The Netherlands* followed Britain's example, using a portrait of King William III on the first issue in 1852, distinguished by the words Post and Zegel in the upper corners. The tiny phosphate island of *Nauru* in the Pacific first used British stamps overprinted NAURU (1916) when a British mandate was established. The colonial island of *Nevis* first issued stamps in 1861, the design being a reference to a medicinal spring on the island. In 1903 Nevis joined St Christopher to form the colony of St Kitts-Nevis which also embraced Anguilla. With no king to portray on its stamps, *Chile*, in 1853, adopted Christopher Columbus and used portraits of him for nearly 60 years. Although *Greenland* was, until 1953, a Danish colony it had no internationally valid stamps of its own until 1938 when stamps portraying King Christian X were issued. Since 1953 Greenland has been an integral part of Denmark, but has continued to issue its own stamps.

[Above] *Ascension*, a dependency of the colony of St Helena, first issued stamps of the 'parent' colony overprinted ASCENSION (1922). Stamps of Bermuda, suitably overprinted, provided *Gibraltar's* first issue (1886). In 1951, the *United Nations* headquarters in New York issued internationally valid stamps of its own. In 1966 Basutoland, an African kingdom under British protection, changed its name to *Lesotho* and featured King Moshoeshoe II on its stamps.

The world's most valuable stamp is the 1¢ black on magenta of 1856 issued by *British Guiana*, of which only this example has ever been found. Despite its poor condition and unattractive design, it realized £166,660 ($280,000) in a New York auction in 1970. The first issue of independent *Israel* (1948), consisting of nine stamps (ranging from 3 milliemes to 1,000 milliemes), illustrated ancient Jewish coins. The first issue of 1884 from *Macao* featured the crown then common to all Portuguese colonial stamps. *Nicaragua's* first stamps (1862) illustrate the volcanic nature of this Central American republic.

The first stamps of *Sarawak* (1869) portrayed the ruling white rajah Sir James Brooke, hence the initials, J(ames B(rooke) R(ajah of) S(arawak) on the corners. Australia became responsible for *Christmas Island*, in the Indian Ocean, under a mandate after World War II. The first stamps

(1958) were Australian, overprinted and re-valued in Singapore cents and dollars. Until 1920 *Liechtenstein* relied on Austria to deal with its postal affairs. The first distinctive stamps (1912) were inscribed *Fürstentum Liechtenstein* and *K.K. Oesterr. Post*. New Zealand constituted its Antarctic Territories as the *Ross Dependency* and first issued distinctive stamps in 1957.

# The Envelope
# Tells the Story

Practically everybody who receives a letter from abroad glances at the stamp on the envelope, tears off the corner with the stamp and throws the rest away as waste paper. A stamp collector, however, looks twice before destroying the envelope. He knows that there may be unusual postal markings either cancelling the stamp itself or applied to the envelope for a particular purpose.

For example, a letter posted on board a British liner would have British stamps on it but the postmark would be that of the next port of call at which mails were put ashore, and it could be Durban in South Africa, or any one of hundreds of the world's ports. At the landing point the British stamp would be cancelled with the town postmark and the word 'paquebot', thus according with the provisions of the Universal Postal Union. Mail franked in this way is forwarded to the addressee anywhere in the world without further charge.

Before the U.P.U. was set up in 1874, the international acceptance of one country's stamps on letters crossing several frontiers before reaching a distant addressee was subject to a series of complicated postal treaties. Earlier still, before stamps were used at all, international mails were virtually non-existent, each letter writer having to fend largely for himself. The postal markings on old stampless letters tell the postal history student how a letter has been handled on its journey across the world. For instance, a son who had settled in one of the new American colonies sending a letter to England could only prepay the letter to the eastern seaboard, and a mark indicating that this prepayment had been made would be put on the letter. At Boston the letter would be handed over to the captain of an England-bound vessel. On arrival the captain would hand over the letter to the post office at the first English port, where it would be stamped 'Ship Letter' together with the name of the port. Irrespective of its final destination the letter would then go to London where the postage in England was calculated. This consisted of one penny for the captain, the charge for bringing the letter to London for assessment, and that for sending it to the addressee, who then paid on delivery.

The haphazard system of carrying mail in all private ships was not very satisfactory and the British post office set up a fleet of speedy, armed 'packet' ships on the well-used routes across the Channel and to and from the West Indies. Letters carried on these ships were endorsed 'packet letter' on arrival in England and the addressee was charged more for their speed and security. There were special arrangements for soldiers and sailors serving abroad and for letters carried by ships of the East India Co. As special postmarks were used for each class of mail, each postmark tells its own story.

The postal reform of 1840 and the introduction of postage stamps led to the introduction of the envelope. In fact, a prepaid envelope was at first favoured by the reformers in preference to stamps. Thus was born the 'Mulready', a curious piece of Victorian design which lasted only a few months.

William Mulready, R.A., was commissioned to design an envelope for the Post Office to put on sale simultaneously with the adhesive stamps. Above the space for the address he drew a figure of Britannia seated with a lion at her feet and her arms flung wide in the act of dispatching winged angels to left and right where standing groups of figures represented the peoples of the expanding British Empire. At the bottom were the words 'Postage One Penny' (the black printing) or 'Postage Two Pence' (the blue printing). When used, the cancellation was a heavy black Maltese Cross postmark which virtually obliterated Britannia. Lampoons soon appeared and the Mulready envelopes were laughed out of existence and replaced by plain envelopes with a printed stamp embossed in the top right corner.

The Golden Jubilee of the Uniform Penny Post was commemorated by the Post Office in 1890 by the issue of stationery marking separate exhibitions at the Guildhall and at the South Kensington Museum. The latter was very quickly parodied by the Postmen's Union whose members thought that the best way to observe the Golden Jubilee was to give them a good pay rise rather than spend the money on public celebrations.

A simple-looking envelope can be the evidence of some great achievement. Letters carried across the world during the development of international air services by pilots in insecure old 'crates' using their wits to defy the worst nature could do to hamper delivery of the mail are real pieces of history, and pieces that might be discarded, unrecognized, without the knowledge of the dates of the flights, the staging points on the routes and other information which the postmarks alone provide.

There are in existence just 50 envelopes which accompanied Sir Francis Chichester on his single-handed epic voyage round the world. The intention had been that they should be posted at his first port of call as 'paquebot' letters, bearing English stamps, but since international postal regulations did not provide for the handling of mail from a private vessel such as *Gypsy Moth IV*, the letters had to have an Australian stamp added and were postmarked at Sydney to provide evidence of arrival there. When Sir Francis eventually put in at Plymouth on 28 May 1967 the British stamps originally fixed to the envelopes were cancelled to complete the record of their unique travels.

[Left] The introduction of the Uniform Penny Post in 1840 meant that a letter of up to $\frac{1}{2}$oz could be posted to anywhere in Great Britain, including Ireland, for 1d. The words ONE PENNY (or TWO PENCE if the envelope was to take a letter of over $\frac{1}{2}$oz and up to 1 oz) were, in effect, the stamp on the Mulready envelope. This Mulready was sent by Rowland Hill, the father of Uniform Post, to Jacob Perkins at the Fleet Street factory where Perkins was printing the rival adhesive stamps!

[Right] Lampoons of the Mulready envelopes appeared on the scene almost as soon as the originals. This example was by the well-known artist John Leech. One series published by Fores, then of Piccadilly, now of Bond Street, uses the same layout for hunting sketches.

[Left] The rare 1d *Mauritius* 'Post Office' stamp posted on the day of issue, 21 September 1847. The date-stamp SE 21 1847 shows the figure 2 in reverse due to being engraved wrongly. The envelope originally contained an invitation to the Governor's ball.

[Right] In 1890 the Post Office commemorated the Golden Jubilee of Uniform Penny Post with an envelope featuring a mailcoach of 1840, the northern mail train of 1890, a postman of 1840 with postal rates from 4d for a local letter to 2s 6d for a letter to Scotland and a postman of 1890 with the single rate of 1d. For the Postmen's Union, a caricature was drawn by Harry Furniss. It showed an 1890 postman bowed down with letters; the mail train is represented as trucks of gold disappearing into the mouth of the Chancellor of the Exchequer, instead of into the pockets of the postmen as wages. Postally used (with an adhesive in place of the printed stamp as on the official envelope) these caricatures are quite rare.

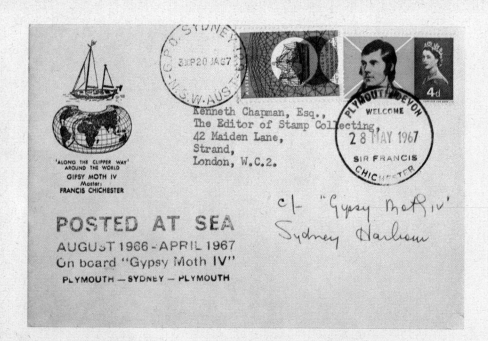

[Left] Only after Sir Francis Chichester returned safely to Plymouth on 28 May 1967 from his solo round-the-world trip was it known that he had carried 50 letters. They were first franked with a British stamp so that they could be posted at any port of call which would treat the letters as 'paquebot' mail – even though it would have been contrary to Universal Postal Union regulations to do so in the case of a private ship. At Sydney, an Australian stamp was added and postmarked, and the letters were readdressed to *Gypsy Moth IV*, Sydney Harbour. When Chichester reached England again the Plymouth Post Office applied the 'welcome' postmark to the English stamp, thus providing evidence of each letter having been carried on the round voyage. The 'posted at sea' cachet, applied when the journey began, assumed Chichester's return in April 1967. Each fortunate recipient of one of these historic envelopes can safely count on having something worth £40 – £50 ($100 – $125) which is likely to increase in value with time.

[Right] During the American Civil War both sides made use of 'patriotic' covers designed to promote support for their respective causes. These varied in style, one of the most popular on the *Union* (Northern) side being similar to that illustrated. The designs of the North incorporated the Union flag of the time with a star for each state in the Union, and mention of the military unit whose member was sending the letter. In this case a Union artilleryman stationed in Wilmington, North Carolina, was writing to his brother at Fort Monroe. Contrary to modern military practice, which allows troops in the field to send letters free of charge, the sender had to pay postage, hence the 3¢ stamp then in use in the Union States. There is no evidence of the customary censorship, probably because the letter was from one soldier to another.

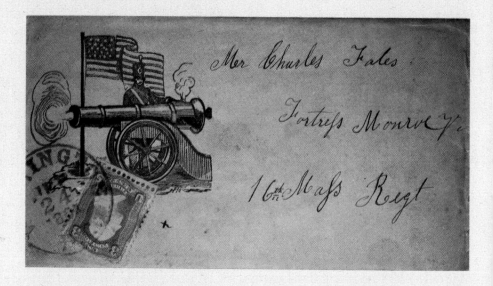

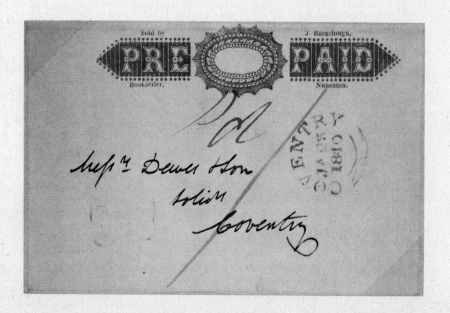

[Left] With the proposed introduction of the prepaid Mulready envelope and folding letter-sheet by the Post Office in May 1840, stationers feared a decline in sales of private envelopes and notepaper. Many privately produced envelopes appeared, of which this Baraclough letter-sheet, published in Nuneaton, is the rarest. Only this example, in the Phillips collection at the National Postal Museum, London, is known. Since it was non-official, the 'prepaid' inscription is misleading: the writer still had to pay one penny postage as indicated by the manuscript 'Pd' and the long l. The uniform penny rate operated from January 1840 (four months before the stamps and Mulready covers appeared), but the public still had to go to a post office and hand over postage in cash. This rare cover was posted on 23 January 1840, during the interim period.

[Right] The opening up of the west in the *United States* brought a need for extending communications. Post office services, often very slow, were soon supplemented by private services, of which the famous Wells Fargo pony express routes were probably the most popular and reliable. Every letter had to be franked with a U.S. stamp which Wells Fargo had officially embossed on their envelopes. The sender paid a further fee varying with distance. In this case the letter was carried to the border where a Canadian stamp was applied to cover postage for the rest of the journey to England. The intrepid pony express riders who maintained communications between the commercial centres of the United States eastern seaboard and the mining camps of the far west and north were well paid for their hazardous work, and postage rates were accordingly high in order to recoup their employers.

[Left] A rare use of the 2d Mulready envelope which was only intended for inland post. This cover was posted at Clifton on 14 November 1840 (by which time the Mulreadys, although still valid, had been withdrawn). The addition of five 2d blue stamps of 1840 bought the total postage up to one shilling, the proper rate at the time for a $\frac{1}{2}$oz letter to *Malta*. The red Maltese Cross postmark was applied at Bristol Head Office. Sub-offices, often little more than receiving houses, were not allowed to cancel the stamps on a letter. They might apply their office hand-stamp to the front or, more usually, the back of the envelope to indicate the actual place of posting and the local head office cancelled the stamps when it received the letter. With the introduction of the Mulready envelope and the 1d and 2d stamps the Maltese cross cancellations, of which there are several varieties, came into use.

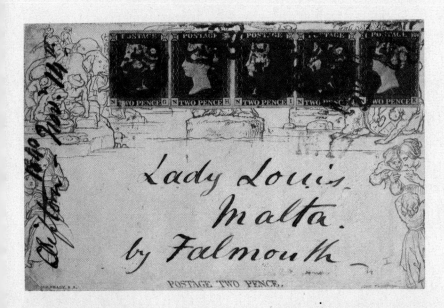

[Right] During the British postal strike in early 1971, hundreds of privately organized local postal services were licensed temporarily by the Post Office which allowed them to issue their own, often rather crude, stamps. Incoming mail from overseas was at first discouraged and, finally, refused for the duration of the strike. To beat this ban, the *Rhodesian* Post Office made arrangements for mail to be flown from Salisbury to London. At the airport it was met by a local postal service representative who undertook to deliver it in Great Britain. The 'Emergency Mail Service' hand-stamp and the additional 50¢ stamp show that this air letter, posted at Mazoe, Rhodesia, reached the addressee through this special service. Two other Commonwealth territories organized 'strike' services and issued special stamps. Malawi overprinted a stamp 'Special United Kingdom Delivery Service', and this was used to supplement the normal airmail charges and pay for the local postal service on arrival in London. The Cook Islands made a similar arrangement and issued two overprinted stamps.

[Above] In 1969 *Anguilla* in the West Indies broke away from the former colony of St Kitts-Nevis-Anguilla when it assumed statehood. St Kitts ceased postal communications with the rebel island and Anguilla blotted out the three-part name on its very limited supplies of stamps, overprinting them 'Independent Anguilla'. Mail was despatched via nearby St Thomas in the U.S. Virgin Islands. The envelope illustrated was posted on 10 November 1969 and arrived in London on 15 November.

[Right] On 16 October 1965, Winifred George, sub-postmistress at the tiny village of Moulton Chapel, Lincolnshire, was attacked by intruders and died. A temporary office was set up in the church hall. The Moulton Chapel hand-stamp and printed registration labels were 'frozen' during investigations, and registered mail was cancelled 'Spalding, Lincs' coded 'W', and emergency registration labels had the name inscribed in manuscript.

[Left] *America*'s first stamp was a 5¢ portraying President Washington, issued by the Postmaster of New York in 1845 for local use only; it was in fact actually inscribed New York. Letters beyond the city boundary were normally paid for in cash at a higher rate which varied according to distance. This very rare cover shows a joined pair of the 5¢ stamps, cancelled as was the custom by the initials of the postal clerk, which constituted prepayment to the address in North Carolina. These stamps are very rare on cover and even when found 'loose' are seldom in good condition because so many old-time collectors around the 1860s made a habit of glueing their stamps into the album, and the heavy gum they used has perished the stamps which are very difficult to salvage intact from old collections.

[Right] A few years before World War II the air routes linking the most distant parts of the British Empire with Great Britain were expanding rapidly, and by 1933 a London-to-Singapore route was opened via the Persian Gulf and India. Illustrated is one of the few commercial covers carried on the inaugural flight from *Kuwait* onwards to *Singapore*. Kuwait, then operating an agency of the Indian Post Office, overprinted Indian stamps for use on the service.

[Below] A cover from *Spain* apparently franked with 'stamps' of the Royal Bulgarian Post! In fact, the stamps, issued in aid of Bulgarian exiles in Spain, have no postal value or significance. The requisite postage of 14 pesetas has been paid by the meter franking. The portrait is that of ex-King Simeon of Bulgaria.

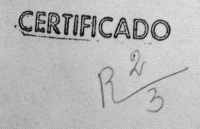

Mr. K. F. Chapman, Chairman
British Philatelic Association
3 Berners Street
LONDON W.1.

[Right] In 1959 the *Scots* requested a stamp to commemorate the centenary of the birth of Robert Burns but the honour was denied. Five years later they reacted sharply to an issue of Shakespeare quater-centenary stamps. This cover, referring to Shakespeare as 'an alien poet', was posted in Edinburgh on the day the Shakespeare stamp appeared, 23 April 1964, the 400th anniversary of the birth of the bard.

We regret featuring Shakespeare, an alien poet, having had denied to us the privilege of similarly honouring our own
ROBERT BURNS

K.F.Chapman Esq.
Editor,
Stamp Collecting
42 Maiden Lane
Strand
LONDON W.C.2

[Right] This very ordinary-looking envelope passed through what was called the Green Cross service between *Great Britain* and Malta during World War II. After the besieged forces on Malta complained of long delays in the delivery of letters from home, the Post Office and the Army agreed on a special form of express mail to boost morale. Troops in Malta were supplied with stickers bearing a green cross to send their relatives, with instructions to put them on their letters to Malta, which were then treated as express letters and given preferential treatment by the Post Office. The test of genuineness is that the sticker is on an envelope addressed to a serviceman in Malta and that it is franked with a 1½d stamp instead of the civilian letter rate of 2½d. Although many thousands of letters went through the service, very few envelopes have survived because they were surrendered during an intensive waste paper salvage drive in Malta. made necessary by the siege conditions.

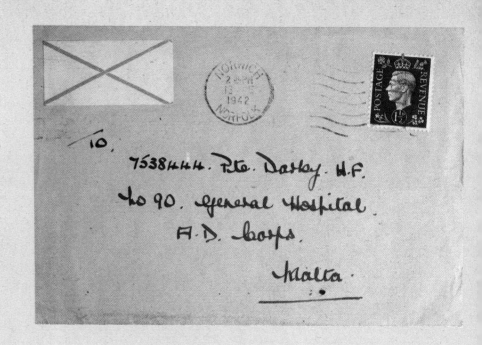

[Left] A *German* field-service postcard addressed by a sergeant on active service to his wife in the early days of World War II. Postage was free but a printed caricature of the British Prime Minister, Neville Chamberlain, appeared as a stamp inscribed 'Not worth a Pfennig'. It was a 'tilt' at Britain and served as a morale booster to the German troops. A similar 'feldpost' card caricatured Sir Winston Churchill who was then First Lord of the Admiralty. It showed Churchill in uniform as an Admiral, his cockaded 'hat' being a battleship broken in two over his head and containing the initials W.C. on the prow. These cards were issued free to troops in the field and also sold to (but not usable by) civilians in aid of German war charities. A third card was issued later with a caricature of Stalin, when Germany attacked her former ally. All these cards are scarce and the one of Stalin is rare. Collectors should beware of later imitations headed 'Feldpostkarte'.

[Right] When *Czechoslovakia* was invaded by Russia in 1968, the German border was sealed by the Russians, and postal traffic ceased. This envelope, containing a letter from a member of the Granada TV newsteam sent out to cover the invasion, was smuggled out of Prague and posted when it was over the border. The red cachet was a bit of anti-Soviet propaganda prepared by the Czechs in defiance of the invaders, and is one of several similar anti-Soviet propaganda cachets. The postmark of Nuremburg is accounted for by the fact that the letter could not be posted in Czechoslovakia since all foreign mail services were stopped by the Russians for the time being.

[Left] The story of the Creation is told here by a first-day cover with the Jewish New Year stamps of 1965, issued by *Israel*. The six days of the Creation, as recounted in the Book of Genesis, are symbolized in the designs of the stamps which represent, [right to left] light, heaven, earth, the stars in the firmament, birds and beasts, and man. This is an example of the way a set of stamps can tell a story in sequence. The cover has little postal history significance other than that it was posted on the day the stamps were issued. First-day covers of this kind are now popular with many collectors and certainly have the merit that they present the complete set in used condition. On the other hand, it is evident that they do not represent the proper postal use of the stamps since they are usually in excess of the postage actually required.

[Right] In May 1910, a new 2d stamp was being printed for the then current King Edward VII issue. Known as 'the Tyrian plum' on account of its colour, the intention was that it should replace the existing 2d green and carmine stamp. On 5 May 1910, one of the new stamps was used by the Post Office, as a matter of courtesy, on an envelope addressed to H.R.H. The Prince of Wales, who was a noted philatelist. By the time the letter was delivered at Marlborough House on 6 May, the King had died, and the addressee had become His Majesty, King George V, in succession to his father. The stamp was never issued, and this is the only example ever used. A few unused examples are known, having come from a limited distribution to important officials. The royal collection, which is now a family heirloom, contains many unique items but no single stamp or cover among the many thousands in the collection can have made a more poignant appeal to the founder of the collection, King George V, than this item which bridged the gap between his being Prince of Wales and becoming the monarch.

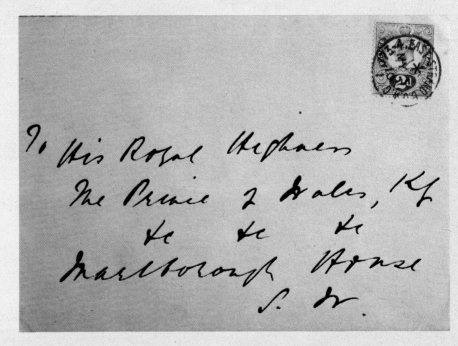

[Left] The first official air mail service in the *United Kingdom* formed part of the celebrations for the coronation of King George V and Queen Mary in 1911. A series of flights took place between the old Hendon Aerodrome in North London and Windsor, the first being on 9 September 1911. Special cards and envelopes were printed and sold to aid charities. The flights carrying mail continued until 16 September. The special 'Aerial Post' stationery sold to the general public was printed in brown and in green, while a limited number of envelopes and cards were printed (as here) in violet and supplied to privileged persons only. The 'public' issue of the cards and envelopes were on sale in nine large London department stores, at the Hendon Aerodrome and the offices of the Aerial Post in Aldwych where they could be posted in special boxes. A number of commercial concerns ranging from *Punch* to Nobel's Explosives Co. Ltd had cards printed with advertisements.

# Postal History on Stamps

Many collectors think of postal history as being concerned solely with old letters and the postmarks they bore before the days of the adhesive stamps. In fact, postal history is a living subject and a continuing study which embraces modern developments such as the use of franking meter machines which make stamps unnecessary.

It was explained in the preceding chapter how the interest in postal history material frequently depends on postal markings which have little pictorial appeal but which mean so much to the postal historian. Stamp collectors who are uninterested in old letters themselves have the best of both worlds since many stamps picture aspects of postal history in a more attractive fashion. Old post offices, cancellations used in exceptional circumstances, modern methods of mail handling and stamps themselves have all found a place in designs which can be arranged to demonstrate the development of postal systems in various parts of the world.

A comprehensive, straightforward thematic collection of stamps can illustrate the story of the introduction of stamps throughout the world on a chronological basis. Those designs associated with postal services add variety to the collection and interest to the story. Old mail coaches, modern postal buses, the functioning of the postal system have all been illustrated to some extent on stamps themselves and can prompt the collector to make a deeper study of any aspect of the postal story which especially appeals to him. Although, perhaps, only a minor aspect of postal history, the uniforms worn by postmen at various periods are not without interest. Some of the bygone postilions were most gloriously apparelled and there are many stamps showing these uniforms in full colour.

Another aspect of the postal service is the introduction of the electric telegraph, using Morse code signals for speedy communications. This, in turn, was followed by wireless telegraphy. Both subjects can be illustrated by stamps as can the development of marine cable services. The ultimate in telecommunications is the relaying of messages by satellite now very fully dealt with on stamps which can be appropriately included in a space thematic collection or added to a collection devoted to postal history on stamps.

[Left] In 1888 *Botswana* (the former Bechuanaland) established a pioneer Native Runner Post between Mafeking and Gubulawayo. Four stamps, issued in 1972, trace the route and illustrate, on separate stamps, the rare postmark used at Gubulawayo; one of the contemporary stamps; two of the runners; and the 'Mafeking killer' postmark used at the end of the route.

[Right] In the top row are a Dummer packet letter from *Jamaica*, dated 1705, and a view of the General Post Office in Kingston in 1820, on stamps for the tercentenary of the island's postal service. The three modern *Spanish* stamps illustrate old issues with appropriate regional cancellations. The *Tristan da Cunha* cancellation on British stamps was as used on mail for the Shackleton-Rowatt expedition of 1921. The two *Italian* stamps were publicity urging the use of postal codes by the public. *Jersey's* 'first day cover' stamps heralded the inauguration of the independent Jersey Post Office in 1969, the stamp on the cover being a miniature of the stamps for which the cover was printed! On one of a series issued in *Mauritius* in 1970 featuring scenes in Port Louis 100 years ago, the post office at which the famous 1847 'Post Office' issue of Mauritius was sold to the public is seen together with a 2d blue 'Post Office'. In 1966 *Malawi* (formerly Nyasaland, and earlier still, British Central Africa) commemorated the 75th anniversary of the B.C.A. postal service by issuing stamps reproducing the 6d British South Africa Co. stamp overprinted B.C.A., as used in the territory in 1891. A selection of *Fijian* stamps spans a century of stamp issuing. The C R monogram on the blue stamp of 1871 was that of King Cakabau who ceded the islands to Britain in 1874. A *Czech* stamp of 1920 was reproduced on the Czechoslovakia 1970 Stamp Day issue.

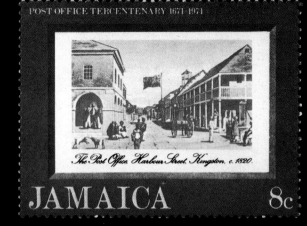

POST OFFICE TERCENTENARY 1671-1971

*Dummer Packet Letter, 1705*

**JAMAICA** 3c

POST OFFICE TERCENTENARY 1671-1971

*The Post Office, Harbour Street, Kingston, c. 1820.*

**JAMAICA** 8c

1'50 PTAS

FRANCO SEIS CUARTOS
CORREOS
A. 3 1851

DIA MUNDIAL DEL SELLO 1969

CORREOS

**ESPAÑA**
F.N.M.T.

50th ANNIVERSARY of the SHACKLETON-ROWETT EXPEDITION

TRISTAN DA CUNHA

SIX PENCE SIX PENCE

7½P

**TRISTAN da CUNHA**

POSTE ITALIANE

7000 BARI 1 VII 1967 CENTRO

*Sig via 56100 Pisa*

CODICE AVVIAMENTO POSTALE

L.50

I.P.S. - ROMA 1966          D. FERRINI

3'50 PTAS

6 REALES
CORREOS
SERENA

DIA MUNDIAL DEL SELLO 1968

CORREOS

**ESPAÑA**
F.N.M.T.

JERSEY POST OFFICE FIRST DAY COVER

JERSEY OCT. 1969 FIRST DAY OF ISSUE

*To Friends of all Nations — GREETINGS!*

INAUGURAL STAMP ISSUE

1'6 INAUGURATION OF THE JERSEY POST OFFICE, 1969 **JERSEY**

SELLAR                    · HARRISON

POSTE ITALIANE

7000 BARI 1 VII 1967 CENTRO

*Sig via 56100 Pisa*

CODICE AVVIAMENTO POSTALE

L.25

I.P.S. - ROMA 1966          D. FERRINI

3'50 PTAS

CERTIF.º DIEZ REALES
CORREOS
CORVERA

DIA MUNDIAL DEL SELLO 1969

CORREOS

**ESPAÑA**
F.N.M.T.

POSTAGE
POST OFFICE TWO PENCE MAURITIUS

GENERAL POST OFFI...

POST OFFICE BUILDING BEFORE 1870

**5c MAURITIUS**

75th ANNIVERSARY OF THE POSTAL SERVICE

BRITISH SOUTH AFRICA COMPANY

B.C.A.

JUSTICE FREEDOM COMMERCE

SIX PENCE

**MALAWI 9d**

1870 – 1970

FIJI

**fiji** 15c

CENTENARY of the FIRST FIJI POSTAGE STAMPS

18-12-1970

1 kčs

**ČESKOSLOVENSKO**

den československej poštovej známky

**5<sup>d</sup>**

Philympia 1970

1840 first engraved issue

**9<sup>d</sup>**

Philympia 1970

1847 first embossed issue

**5<sup>c</sup>**

THE WORLDS RAREST STAMP

Guyana
SOUTH AMERICA

**1/6**

Philympia 1970

1855 first surface printed issue

CONVEYANCE COMPANY LTD · FIRST POSTAL SERVICE
1872 — 1972

CENTENARY OF ST.LUCIA STEAM

Caribbean Sea

Castries

St. Lucia

Soufrière

Atlantic Ocean

HEWANORRA INTERNATIONAL AIRPORT

**ST. LUCIA**  **5 CENTS**

**1870** ST.KITTS STAMP CENTENARY **1970**

50 CENTS

ST·KITTS A SP 12 71

AN EARLY POSTMARK

SIX PENCE

**ST.CHRISTOPHER · NEVIS · ANGUILLA**

CENTENARY OF ST.LUCIA STEAM CONVEYANCE COMPANY LTD.

FIRST POSTAL  SERVICE 1872

1872 **50 CENTS** 1972

**ST. LUCIA**

**1870** ST.KITTS STAMP CENTENARY **1970**

ONE PENNY

G.P.O. ST.KITTS 1970

**½ CENT**

**ST.CHRISTOPHER · NEVIS · ANGUILLA**

TAG DER BRIEFMARKE 1972

**4<sup>S</sup> +1<sup>S</sup>**

REPUBLIK ÖSTERREICH

A.PILCH  1972  W.PFEILER

**THE GAMBIA**  **4<sup>d</sup>**

GAMBIA

FOUR PENCE

CENTENARY OF FIRST POSTAGE STAMPS  1869 - 1969

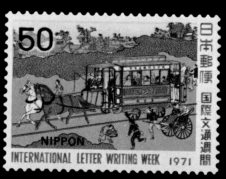

**50**

NIPPON

INTERNATIONAL LETTER WRITING WEEK 1971

[This page] *Britain's* – and the world's – first stamp, the engraved Penny Black, together with the first issues, both surface printed and embossed, were featured on the commemorative issue – Philympia – of 1970. *St Lucia's* first stamps were issued in 1870 for local use on ship mail. *Fiji's* 1870 issue were local stamps printed by the 'Fiji Times Express'. A life-size reproduction of the world's most expensive stamp was a natural choice for *Guyana*. A Viennese letter-carrier, the *Mauritius* mail coach and *Japanese* postal horse bus all represent facets of the postal service.

MAURITIUS MAIL COACH 1870

**50 c  MAURITIUS**

**1870**  **fiji**

FIJI TIMES EXPRESS

TIMES EXPRESS

**1 PENNY.**

**6 PENCE.**

1870 CENTENARY of the FIRST FIJI POSTAGE STAMPS  **4<sup>c</sup>**

[This page] The *German* inflation of 1923 is reflected in this block of nine 20,000,000,000 mark stamps which franked a small packet at a total cost of 180,000,000,000 marks. The posting, sorting and delivery of a letter is shown in sequence by the Japanese stamps commemorating, in 1971, the centenary of *Japan's* national postal service. *Jersey* recalls the Paris Siege of 1870 when letters were carried out of beleaguered Paris and across the Prussian lines by balloon. The letter illustrated on the stamp is one that was addressed to Jersey and is usually considered to be the first piece of airmail delivered to the island, albeit only after a landfall of balloons outside Paris. The only American issue ever printed in England was that for the Confederate States during the Civil War, the printers being De La Rue, whose founder was a Guernseyman. The post-code symbol on the small *Japanese* stamp is part of an annual series educating the public to use postal codes on mail. Stamp collecting, recognized in the U.S. as a major hobby, was given a boost by the 8¢ stamp issued in 1972 for general use.

# Commemorative Stamps

For almost 50 years after stamps first appeared they were regarded by the post offices which issued them, and by the public who used them, as utility articles. They were stuck on to letters to pay postage and, once cancelled by the postmark, they ceased to have any function other than to interest a small band of collectors.

In 1888, New South Wales took the first timorous step towards commemorative stamps. A new series of definitive stamps was commissioned. A break from the ubiquitous portrait of Queen Victoria was decided upon and the resulting stamps showed a view of Sydney; a portrait of Captain James Cook; an emu; a lyre bird; a kangaroo; a map of Australia; portraits of Captain Arthur Phillip, the first Governor, and Lord Carrington, the Governor in 1888 (a rare departure from practice in that it portrayed a living person other than the monarch); and, on one value only (the 6d), a contemporary portrait of Queen Victoria above the arms of the colony. The important feature, however, was that each stamp carried the inscription 'One Hundred Years', a gentle reminder that it was in 1788 that Governor Phillip had established the first Australian colony at Sydney Cove.

The first full-blooded commemorative series came from the United States in 1893 when the Columbian Exposition at Chicago celebrated the fourth centenary of the landing of Christopher Columbus. The issue consisted of 16 stamps ranging from 1 cent to 5 dollars. The designs were taken from paintings and engravings concerned with the historic voyages of Columbus. It is the perfect example of the way a single stamp issue can tell a dramatic story. It was also the perfect example of how a government, which soon learned its lesson, tried to exploit the philatelist and failed dismally. While a few wealthy collectors and Columbus fans bought an entire set for $16.32 as souvenirs, the stamps remained a drug on the philatelic market until the late 1920s. The great expansion of the hobby since then has brought about the inevitable rise in value, as commemorative stamps have become an accepted part of philatelic life and a straight mint set of these 1893 Columbians (ignoring shade variations and the very rare 4¢ error of colour –

itself worth over £1,000 [$2,500]) now costs anything up to £500 ($1,250) depending on its condition.

Happily, few commemorative sets have gone so far out of reach, and there are now thousands of issues celebrating events of international, national, or even local, importance available to all, each with a story to tell.

Commemorative stamps can be included in a collection of other stamps from one country, taking their place among the other issues of the country concerned on a chronological basis; or they can be grouped as a separate section and arranged in a sequence that demonstrates the story of the events they commemorate, almost as an illustrated history book might do. A third method is to ignore the country of origin and collect stamps showing the interlocking stories of countries which share common experiences or a similar culture.

Certain events of international importance result in stamps from many different countries to commemorate them. An obvious example is the Olympic Games. West Germany naturally issued stamps for the Munich Olympics, including an imaginative miniature sheet of four stamps, which, with the sheet margins, gave an aerial view of the setting of the magnificent stadium in which most of the events were held, thus providing an ideal frontispiece for a collection of the stamps of all nations which supported the games.

The issuing of stamps to commemorate current and past events has become a matter of national prestige. They throw light on the history of long-established nations, or the aspirations of emergent peoples are brought to the notice of a world-wide audience at a minimum cost, since these miniature posters pay for themselves when used as postage stamps and may even produce a substantial philatelic revenue without being called on to perform any postal duty.

It is exceptional nowadays for any commemorative issue to include unnecessary high-value stamps. Postal administrators realize that collectors prefer to obtain the stamps in complete sets which tell the full story and are willing to buy them when there is less strain on their pockets than was the case with America's Columbus blockbuster of 1893.

[Opposite] In 1970, 200 years after Captain James Cook and his companions stepped ashore on the eastern coast of *Australia* and claimed the new land for the Crown, the event was commemorated by that country with these five joined stamps, the Cook bicentenary issue. In addition to Cook himself and several of his companions, the design includes their ships and navigational tools; a map of Botany Bay; a kangaroo and a drawing of the banksia. Earlier and later issues concerned with Cook's voyages add to the story and provide the nucleus of a collection.

[This page] Over the centuries, *Britain* has dispatched explorers to every continent other than Europe. In 1972 and 1973 the British Post Office issued nine portrait stamps honouring just a few of the more famous of the explorers. The 1972 issue concentrated on leading figures of polar exploration: James Clark Ross, who, in the early 1800s explored both the Arctic and Antarctic – the Ross Sea is his geographical memorial; Martin Frobisher, the first Briton in the Arctic Circle, seeking the North West Passage in 1576; Henry Hudson, who in 1610 got as far as Hudson

Bay; and Robert Falcon Scott, who reached the South Pole in 1910. The 1973 issue marked principally the centenary of the death of David Livingstone in central Africa in 1873, with a joined pair of 3p stamps that linked him with Henry Stanley Morton, who found Livingstone at Ujiji in 1871. Sir Francis Drake, who pioneered circumnavigation of the globe, is included with Sir Walter Raleigh, explorer of the West Indies and North America, and Charles Sturt, the man who went to Australia and was responsible for opening up vast areas in the east.

23

It is an *American* practice to issue stamps not only to commemorate anniversaries but also to honour national institutions. This selection of U.S. stamps includes both categories, with tributes paid to early flight by the 'Jupiter' balloon stamp and to modern space technology by the Robert Goddard Atlas rocket stamp. The Homemakers stamp, patterned on an old sampler, and American Music and Fine Arts and the Trumbull stamps represent cultural activities past and present. The Mail Order Centenary celebrates a basic element in American life, the purchasing of goods by post. Statehood anniversaries have provided the reason for many American commemorative stamps. A collection of them arranged in chronological order of the achievement of statehood clearly demonstrates the westward thrust over the years and development of the U.S. federal system. More modern achievements are represented by the stamps commemorating the opening in 1964 of the Verrazano Narrows Bridge, linking Brooklyn and Staten Island in New York harbour.

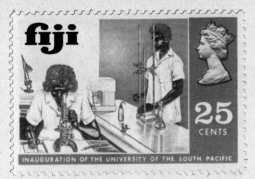

The scene of the Great Fire of London in 1666 finds a place on the *St Helena* stamp because a number of Londoners who lost everything in the fire emigrated to the tiny South Atlantic island colony the following year, and the tercentenary of their arrival was commemorated by St Helena in 1967. The *Fiji* stamp is a 'current event' commemorative marking the inauguration of the University of the South Pacific. The Accountants' Congress stamp from *Australia* links the professional figure work with computer accounting. *Germany* and *France* issued similar stamps in 1973 to mark the tenth anniversary of their Treaty of Co-operation. The attractive Greek stamp marks a Congress of the Greek – American Progressive Association. An International Slavonic Congress in 1968 accounts for the illuminated letter 'S' on the stamp from *Czechoslovakia*. The *Netherlands*' fourteenth census resulted in a somewhat severe design and again introduces a computer element in the lower left corner. *Italy* is represented by a centenary stamp for its famous Alpine Corps and a Silver Jubilee commemorative for its national airline. International Education Year was commemorated by *Lebanon*, and *Colombia* used modern symbolism on the stamp for the twentieth anniversary of the Intergovernmental Committee for European Immigrants.

[Left] Four examples of typical *American* flora appropriately mark a botanists' eleventh International Botanical Congress held in 1969. [Below] Three aviation events are commemorated on stamps from *Italy*, the 25th anniversary of Alitalia; *Fiji*, the 40th anniversary of the first trans-Pacific flight by Kingsford-Smith, Ulm, Warner and Lyons (portrayed below Kingsford-Smith's famous Southern Cross aircraft), and, in contrast, one of *Great Britain*'s issue to celebrate the maiden flight of Concorde. The 350th anniversary of the founding of the *Colombian* city of Bucaramanga avoided a commonplace view of the city in 1622 by a modern approach in design. In 1973 *Japan* welcomed back the Ryukyu Islands from American administration by a single 20 yen stamp illustrating the Gate of Courtesy set in a framework of bingata folkweave. An alpine climber is seen on one of *Italy*'s issue for the centenary of the Trentine Alpinists Society. A representative and varied selection indicates the wide-ranging nature of commemorative designs.

*San Marino* is inclined to produce stamps on the slightest pretext, but few collectors quibbled at the issue in 1969 of a series of nine stamps in memory of Walt Disney. These three show Donald Duck, Mickey Mouse and Walt Disney with Baghera and Mowgli from Disney's 'Jungle Book' film. Disney himself has also appeared on an American stamp and his cartoons on those of other countries.

The turbulent history of the Caribbean is recalled by the *Jamaican* stamp picturing two notorious women pirates, Mary Read and Anne Bonny, with the title page of an account of the trial they faced in company with several male companions. *Argentine's* contribution is an Aviation and Space Week stamp. *Uruguay* offers a few bars – with words – of her national anthem and *Ghana* commemorates the Silver Jubilee of the Cocoa Research Institute on whose work her welfare largely depends. The 150th anniversary of the deciphering of the hieroglyphic inscriptions on the Rosetta Stone by the French Professor Champollion, which furthered the study of language of ancient Egypt, was commemorated by *France* and *Egypt* in 1972. Other anniversaries and events are the centenary of *Austria's* University of Agriculture (featuring its coat of arms), the R.S.P.C.A. and the 150th anniversary of the Macquarie Lighthouse in *Australia*, 50 years of the Royal British Legion (*Jersey*), a Council of Europe Art Exhibition (*Malta*) and the opening of *Botswana's* National Museum.

350th ANNIVERSARY OF THE LANDING OF SIR THOMAS WARNER **40 CENTS**
BUILDING THE FORT AT 'OLD ROAD'
St. CHRISTOPHER NEVIS ANGUILLA

VAN GOGH
**REPUBLIQUE TOGOLAISE**
INDUSTRIALISATION DU TOGO — TEXTILE DE DADJA
**20F**
SHAMIR

**60**
HONG KONG **10¢**
Diamond Jubilee
1911-1971
念紀禧鑽軍童
角壹港香

E II R **10¢**
**MONTSERRAT**

SCAUTISMO
POSTE ITALIANE L.50
IAS·ROMA·1968 — C.FONTANI

Antarctic Treaty 1961-1971
**10p**
British Antarctic Territory

KONGRESS DER GEMEINWIRTSCHAFT
IX. INTERNATIONALER — WIEN 23-25.MAI 1972
6 4
REPUBLIK ÖSTERREICH
A.PILCH 1972 W.SEIDEL

JERSEY 'Battle of Flowers'
1'6
J. TOOMBS — COURVOISIER S.A.

Britain's colonial history is frequently illustrated on stamps, a typical example being the arrival of Sir Thomas Warner in *St Christopher*, West Indies, in 1632. The building of the first wooden fort is represented but the Union Jack as shown did not then exist! The modernization of newly independent African nations is a popular theme for designs; one from the *Togo Republic* has an old-fashioned loom and its automated successor. Scouts and guides crop up regularly on issues for anniversaries, these three examples being from *Hong Kong*, *Montserral* and *Italy*. An example of international cooperation was the Antarctic Treaty of 1961 and the British Antarctic Territory celebrated its tenth anniversary. *Austria* was the scene, in 1972, of the eleventh International Congress Pace, an industrial and economic cooperative movement whose emblem overshadows the famous Hofburg Palace.

**LIBERIA**
**5¢**
PRESIDENT TUBMAN'S VISIT GERMANY 1956
**POSTAGE**

ШЛЕМ
КРЕМЛЬ. ОРУЖЕЙНАЯ ПАЛАТА
1964
**4** ПОЧТА СССР
К

QUINTO CENTENARIO · DIVINA COMMEDIA · EDIZIONE FOLIGNATE

pma parte de quefto libro loquale fechiama inferno : nel quale lautore fa prohemio ad tucto eltractato del libro:.

EL mezo delcamin dinrã uita mi trouai puna felua ofcura che la diricta uia era fmarrita Et quanto adir ãlera cofa dura efta felua feluagia afpra efone che nel penfier renoua la paura

ITALIA L.50
I.P.S.-ROMA-1972

QUINTO CENTENARIO · DIVINA COMMEDIA · EDIZIONE MANTOVANA

E DANTIS ALIGERII POETAE FLORENTINI INFERNI INCIPIT CA-PITVLVM PRIMVM INCIPIT

ITALIA L.90
I.P.S.-ROMA-1972

QUINTO CENTENARIO · DIVINA COMMEDIA · EDIZIONE JESINA

ITALIA L.180
I.P.S.-ROMA-1972

Deliverance and Patience arrive in Jamestown Virginia 1610

Bermuda 15 CENTS

BERMUDA
350th. Anniversary of Parliament. 1620-1970

FIRST ASSEMBLY HOUSE IN ST. PETER'S CHURCH, ST. GEORGE'S. 1620-1622

18 CENTS

MUTTON SNAPPER
Lutjanus analis
EiiR
RACIAL EQUALITY YEAR-1971
BRITISH HONDURAS
50 cents

OMM WMO
IMO/WMO CENTENARY 1973
UGANDA KENYA TANZANIA
RELEASING OF A WEATHER BALLOON
70 c

AUTONOMOUS METHODIST CHURCH 1967
COASTAL VIEW OF MOUNT COKE AREA
METHODIST CONFERENCE MAY 1969
St.VINCENT
2 c

1970 COMMONWEALTH GAMES
SWAZILAND
25c

For the 500th anniversary of three famous editions of Dante's 'Divine Comedy' *Italy* reproduced the opening sentences from each of them in illuminated manuscript form. *Bermuda* pictures the first settlers arriving from Jamestown, Virginia, in 1610 and its first Assembly House. Overprints are not normally used for commemorative stamps, two of the exceptions being those for Racial Equality Year (1971) in *British Honduras* (now Belize) and the 1969 Methodist Conference of the West Indian Autonomous Methodist Church, over-printed on a normal stamp itself already overprinted. *East Africa* marked the centenary of the World Meteorological Organization (now a U.N. Agency) with stamps one of which shows the release of a weather balloon. The 1970 Common-wealth Games inspired many issues from competing countries, and a stop-watch from *Papua & New Guinea* commemorates the fourth South Pacific Games held at Papee-te, Tahiti, in 1971. *Uruguay* celebrates the round-the-world voyage made by the Alferez Campora.

4th South Pacific Games,
Papua & New Guinea
Papeete 1971
28c

1960-1963
HOMENAJE AL 'ALFEREZ CAMPORA'
CORREO AEREO
1·40 c
URUGUAY
IMP NACIONAL

x

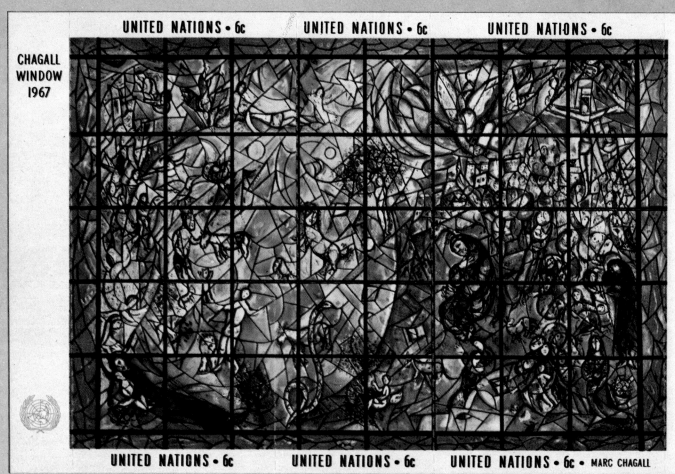

CHAGALL WINDOW 1967

UNITED NATIONS · 6c     UNITED NATIONS · 6c     UNITED NATIONS · 6c

UNITED NATIONS · 6c     UNITED NATIONS · 6c     UNITED NATIONS · 6c · MARC CHAGALL

Each year *Sweden* issues stamps portraying Nobel Prize Award Winners of 60 years earlier. The series began in 1962 when the 1902 prizewinners shared honours on two stamps. In 1966 the *Argentine Republic* commemorated a series of little-known rocket launches in the Antarctic by issuing a stamp showing a map and the 'Centaur' rocket. A very different Argentinian achievement was recalled in 1968 by stamps featuring their most famous medical person- ality, Guillermo Rawson, and the hospital (founded in 1868) named after him. The stylized carrier pigeon from *Czechoslovakia* is a Stamp Day commemorative issue. The window by Marc Chagall in the U.N. head- quarters was reproduced in 1967 as a miniature sheet of stamps which could be broken up into six 6¢ stamps for normal use. The stamps were issued on U.N. Day (24 October) 1967 in support of the Dis- armament Campaign.

WE APPRECIATE
OUR SERVICEMEN

UNITED STATES
SAVINGS BONDS
25TH ANNIVERSARY 5c

National
Park Service
1916-1966
5c
U.S.

GENERAL FEDERATION OF WOMEN'S CLUBS
75 Years
of Service for Freedom
and Growth
UNITED STATES POSTAGE 5c

SESQUICENTENNIAL
INDIANA
1816 1966
5¢
U.S. POSTAGE

Mary
Cassatt
American
Artist
5C
U.S. POSTAGE

《在延安文艺座谈会上的讲话》发表二十五周年

中国人民邮政 8分

النكرى المؤية لتأسيس
الجامعة الأميركية في بيروت
١٩٦٦ - ١٨٦٦

20P
POSTE AERIENNE

CENTENAIRE DE L'UNIVERSITÉ
AMERICAINE DE BEYROUTH
1866 - 1966

LIBAN لبنان

American anniversaries covered by the five *United States* stamps are the 25th anniversary of the first issue, in 1941, of United States Savings Bonds, the 150th anniversary of Indiana's statehood, the Golden Jubilee of the National Park Service, the 75th anniversary (in 1966) of the General Federation of Women's Clubs and a stamp commemorating the work of Mary Cassatt by reproducing her painting, 'The Boating Party'. The fifth World Basketball Championship was celebrated by *Uruguay* in 1967 by five stamps and the miniature sheet (illustrated), this being unusual in that the design extends beyond the confines of the stamp itself. The Silver Jubilee of the publication, in 1942, of Mao Tse-tung's 'Talks on Literature and Art' was duly commemorated in 1972 by the *People's Republic of China*. One of three stamps illustrating part of the text is shown here. American influence in the Middle East is not new for in 1966 Lebanon Commemorated the centenary of the American University of Beirut, founded by the Rev. Daniel Bliss in 1866. An ancient artifact was the *Argentine's* contribution to the twentieth anniversary of Unesco. When the United Nations celebrates an anniversary of one of its agencies, member-countries issue stamps of their own and give the occasion a 'local' flavour dealing with some aspect of the agency's interest. Argentine's example is a native carving of the pre-Spanish days.

XX ANIVERSARIO UNESCO
10
PESOS
R.ARGENTINA
CASA DE MONEDA "I-1967" H. VIOLA DIB.

LOS DIEZ MANDAMIENTOS

CORREO **10** CENTAVOS

**NICARAGUA**

federazione società filateliche
1919 italiane 1969

**ITALIA** L.50

1918 1968

**Conti Correnti Postali**

POSTE ITALIANE L.50

I.P.S.-ROMA 1968 G. BELLI

POSTE **ITALIANE**

56100 Pisa

CODICE AVVIAMENTO POSTALE

L.20

١٩٧١

10 B.
POSTAGE **YEMEN ARAB REPUBLIC**

One of the most unusual subjects for commemoration is seen on eleven stamps from *Nicaragua*: the implementation of the Ten Commandments. The first stamp pictured Moses with the Tablets of the Law (a Rembrandt painting) and the remainder detailed the Commandments, the texts of which are printed on the back of the stamps. The three *Italian* stamps relate, respectively, to 50 years of the Italian Philatelic Federation, the Postal Cheque (Giro) Service of the Italian Post Office and the introduction of postal coding in 1967. Picasso's 'Guernica', a memorial to the ill-fated Spanish town bombed in 1936 by Nazi forces was used by *Czechoslovakia* on the 30th anniversary of the International Brigade's Service in Spain. A death-defying endurance test still undertaken by young men on Pentecost Island in the *New Hebrides* provides three designs showing men jumping from a platform with their ankles tied to thongs attached to the platform and long enough to allow the jumper to land upright. Regional postal unions exist in various parts of the world, supplementing the work of the U.P.U; here is an example from the *Yemen Arab Republic* commemorating the Arab Postal Union.

30. VÝROČÍ MEZI-NÁRODNÍCH BRIGÁD VE ŠPANĚLSKU

**ČESKOSLOVENSKO**

60h

RF THE PENTECOST ISLAND LAND DIVERS EIIR

15
POSTAGE GOLD CENTIMES

**NEW HEBRIDES**
CONDOMINIUM

RF THE PENTECOST ISLAND LAND DIVERS EIIR

25
POSTAGE GOLD CENTIMES

**NEW HEBRIDES**
CONDOMINIUM

RF THE PENTECOST ISLAND LAND DIVERS EIIR

1
POSTAGE GOLD FRANC

**NEW HEBRIDES**
CONDOMINIUM

1697 CANALETTO 1768

POSTE ITALIANE L.50

A selection of fine art reproduced on stamps. [Left] 'Boyhood of Raleigh' (Millais) and 'English Fleet in the Channel' (Monamy), both Jerseymen, hence the *Jersey* stamps; 'Mares and Foals in a Land-scape', one of Stubbs' most famous pictures and 'Children Coming out of School' by L.S. Lowry, from the *British* Post Office; a fresco by Anton Troger in Melk Monastery, one of a series from *Austria* featuring baroque frescoes. [Above] The head of St George, a sculpture by Donatello. [Below] From the Albertina Art Collection in Vienna there is a self-portrait by Rembrandt and (bottom right) 'Young Hare' by Dürer, from an issue marking the bicentenary of the collection. [Right] On the bicentenary of the death of Canaletto, in 1768, a reproduction of his 'St Mark's Square, Venice' was issued by *Italy* (in 1968) and the 450th anniversary of Raphael was similarly observed, in 1970, with stamps showing a detail of his fresco, 'Galatea', and his 'Madonna of the Gold-finch'. Of all the subjects used for stamp designs, the reproduction of famous works of art is a popular choice among both designers and stamp collectors. Most of the classic nativity scenes have appeared on Christmas issues from all over the world; and hundreds of these miniature repro-ductions have appeared on stamps com-memorating birth or death centenaries of the artists concerned. The reproductions vary greatly in quality depending on the printing process used.

ITALIA L.20

1483 RAFFAELLO 1520

ITALIA L.50

1483 RAFFAELLO 1520

REPUBLIK ÖSTERREICH
STIFT MELK

200 Jahre Albertina
REMBRANDT
Republik Österreich

200 Jahre Albertina
DÜRER
Republik Österreich

# Thematic Collecting

Age-old concepts of stamp collecting became out of date with the advent of thematic collecting. No longer was the collector adjured to mount his stamps methodically according to country of origin and then, within each country, in order of issue. The variety of approach and expression afforded to the individual taste, the freedom of action within a self-chosen discipline, has made thematic collecting the quickest-developing side of stamp collecting today. This applies equally to philately on either side of the Atlantic, the only difference being that on the American side the term 'topical' replaces the English-preferred 'thematic'.

Thematically, stamps are collected irrespective of where they come from: it is the subject of the design that matters. There are thousands of stamps illustrating flowers in natural colour and they come from all parts of the world. The stamp collector with botanical or horticultural inclinations can experience no greater pleasure than planning a collection which groups the stamps according to the flower families represented, irrespective of the country of issue. In this way

Flowers have been popular subjects for stamp designs all over the world. Generally speaking the varieties depicted are native to the countries issuing the stamps. Collecting flower stamps is more interesting if the collection is limited to those depicting native flowers. Flowers of the same family from varying regions of the world should be grouped to show how the species is spread, and also how flowers of the same family vary according to where they grow. Naturally, this applies principally to wild flowers from which many 'domestic' varieties have been propagated. Among the examples illustrated, two of the more exotic are the hibiscus and frangipani from the *Cook Islands* while the *Australian* kangaroo paw and the monkey fiddle from the Caribbean bear unfamiliar names.

orchids from Malaysia, South America and elsewhere meet in the stamp album and demonstrate how international the orchid family is. Such an arrangement also quickly isolates those flowers which are indigenous to a particular part of the world, as in the case of the Australian wattle. The botanist will readily recognize flowers which, although bearing different names in widely separated countries, come from the same family.

Over the years, hundreds of stamps have depicted aircraft of all kinds from the days of the Wright Brothers in 1904 through to Concorde. The aviation expert can arrange these to produce a world history of development in aircraft design and efficiency, based on the products of the United Kingdom, the United States, France, Germany and Russia; but the stamps can come from any country whose stamp designs have incorporated these aircraft.

Ecclesiastical architecture ranging from British village churches to the Buddhist temples of Cambodia (now the Khmer Republic) taking in the world's major Christian cathedrals and then mosques of Islam, gives scope for a collection of exceptional interest. It can be arranged according to the religions represented and then be broken down in recognized periods within each religion, the great Renaissance cathedrals being grouped without regard to the country in which they were built.

Journalists can form collections of stamps commemorating the anniversaries of some of the world's greatest newspapers both in the free world and in the countries where the press is now more strictly controlled. Apart from the Press itself, there are many stamps with literary associations. Stamps with portraits of internationally famous authors are plentiful and there are many illustrating scenes from their books.

The Saturday sailor can call upon a wide range of stamps whose designs are concerned with sailing in all parts of the world under all conditions. If the mariner's interests extend beyond sail then the seas are wide open with thousands of stamps featuring ships of all kinds from small river steamers plying on inland waters in West Africa to the great ocean liners, many of them being specific vessels whose histories are recorded. It is also possible to collect stamps of the great naval battles which have taken place in the past.

Stamps with musical associations can be arranged to illustrate the history of European music. All the major composers up to the close of the nineteenth century have appeared on stamps honouring their birth or death and many of the issues include excerpts from some of their best-known works. For those whose interests go beyond Europe there are musical instruments ranging from those which were familiar to King David in biblical times to the extraordinary contraptions like the nzomari used in East Africa to encourage dancing at festivals and the gay steel band from the carnivals of Trinidad.

Among the 350 or so themes listed by the American Topical Association is one which no keen stamp collector will pass lightly – 'Stamps on Stamps'. In 1940 the centenary of Britain's Penny Black was commemorated in several countries and set the pattern for other stamps as their centenaries fell due. Few collectors can afford to buy an 1847 1d Mauritius 'Post Office' at the going price – when it is available – of about £20,000 ($50,000), but all can buy the 1947 issue reproducing this famous rarity and the 2d blue. Similarly, many of the world's classic rare stamps have been incorporated in the designs of commemorative stamps which are not expensive. Such issues can be used as an introduction to a collection of the country concerned or they can be brought together in date order to show how the idea of using stamps spread throughout the world as the years went by during the nineteenth century.

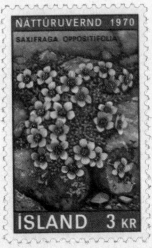

MAURITIUS

MAURITIUS DODO (EXTINCT)

R⁰ 1

Československo
Ledňáček obecný
Alcedo atthis L.

1·20
Kčs

دولة قطر ۲ درهم

POSTAGE

بريد

ALCEDO ATTHIS

2
DIRHAMS

STATE OF
QATAR

MAURITIUS

15 c

PARRAKEET
GROSSE CATEAU VERTE

26 +13
PESOS

TUCAN
GRANDE
(RAMPHASTOS
TOCO)

AEREO

PRO
INFANCIA

R.ARGENTINA

CASA DE MONEDA "XII-1967" A. BOERO Dib.

Birds of the world are another popular theme ranging from the extinct dodo, formerly native to *Mauritius*, to the lively Gorfus penguins found in the Crozet Archipelago of the *French Antarctic Territory*. Again, it is the wild life which is worth studying through stamp designs. As this selection of stamps shows, the pictorial treatment varies widely from the bold design of *Qatar* on the Persian Gulf [top right] to the very delicately engraved *Czech* stamp adjoining it; both feature 'alcedo atthis', one of the kingfisher family. In the case of *Qatar* [bottom right] the peregrine falcon, although wild, is captured and trained for the old art of hawking which is still practised by local sheiks.

The humming bird on the *St Lucia* stamp is one of the smallest and brightly plumed birds found anywhere in the world. There are several other stamps from other countries which feature this attractive bird. The parakeet on the 15¢ *Mauritius* stamp is another colourful bird which turns up on stamps from various parts of the world. The toucan on the *Argentine* stamp is indigenous to South America but comes from the same family as the more familiar woodpecker. The use of bird designs on stamps specifically issued for use on air mail and inscribed accordingly, as in the case of the toucan, is quite usual. Such stamps fit into a thematic collection of birds on stamps or into a collection of air mail stamps, as distinct from a thematic collection of aeroplanes on stamps.

HUMMING BIRD (Colibri)

St LUCIA

25 c

1971

15

日本郵便

NIPPON

第25回 愛鳥週間

1ᵉ SPECIALE VLUCHT

14 FEBRUARI 1946

NEDERLAND - SURINAME - NED. ANTILLEN

SURINAME

25 c

TERRES AUSTRALES ET ANTARCTIQUES
POSTES        FRANÇAISES

RF  ARCHIPEL des CROZET  1 F

دولة قطر ۳ ریالات

POSTAGE

بريد

FALCO PEREGRINUS

3
RIYALS

STATE OF
QATAR

VIỆT NAM
DÂN CHỦ CỘNG HÒA

VỊT LƯỠI LIỀM

ANAS FALCATA

BƯU CHÍNH

12
XU

12
к

ПОЧТА СССР

1972

ОЧКОВАЯ ГАГА

50 CENTS
1929 1968 Dr. MARTIN LUTHER KING
ST. KITTS NEVIS ANGUILLA

1/6
Gandhi
Centenary
Year 1969

25 CENTS ST. LUCIA 25 CENTS
81-CENTENARY OF THE BIRTH OF NAPOLEON 1969

POSTAGE
1 DIRHAM
بعثة أبولو 11 إلى القمر
APOLLO 11 - MOON MISSION
ARMSTRONG
QATAR قطر

NICARAGUA
20¢ AEREO
20¢ FRANKLIN D. ROOSEVELT 1945-1970
XXV ANIVERSARIO DE SU MUERTE

CENTENAIRE DE VATICAN I
20 c
S.S. JEAN XXIII 1958-1963
REPUBLIQUE RWANDAISE

L.v.Beethoven 1770 1970
ΕΛΛΑΣ·HELLAS ΔΡ 4.50

Bertrand Russell
1872-1970
बर्ट्रेंड रसल
भारत INDIA Rs RS 1·45

CHURCHILL
U.S. 5 CENTS

3ᵈ Malta

G.B. SHAW
1856 1950
MARILE ANIVERSARI CULTURALE 19.6
40 BANI POSTA
R.P. ROMINA
ZAINEA S.

1871-1937 1971 ПОЧТА СССР
ЭРНЕСТ РЕЗЕРФОРД
6K

Portraits have featured on stamps since the world's first issues. While it is natural that the head of state, monarch or president, should appear on stamps, this selection is exceptional in that the portraits are those of international figures who have been honoured by countries other than their own. The Gandhi stamp issued by *Great Britain* for the centenary of the birth of a man who suffered imprisonment by the British before his long campaign of civil disobedience gave India her freedom was judged by an Indian panel to be the most successful of the many stamps from all parts of the world issued for the Gandhi centenary. The silhouettes [top right] are those of Napoleon and Josephine on an issue of *St Lucia*, for Napoleon's birth centenary. The most unusual tribute is to find Rutherford, of nuclear fission fame, on a *Russian* stamp.

25 FILS
ABU DHABI أبوظبي

Health stamps cover a wide field of medical research and volunteer labour involving many persons and organizations. Personalities represented here include the Doctors Mayo whose *American* clinic became a byword for healing, and Professor Christiaan Barnard, the South African heart transplant pioneer who is seen (together with the Groote Schuur Hospital where the first transplant was carried out) on a *South African* stamp, the initials RSA (Republic of South Africa) being sufficient to identify the country under the Universal Postal Union regulations. Dr. Elizabeth Gunn was the founder of the *New Zealand* health camps for under-privileged children. This Elizabeth Gunn stamp, issued in 1969, marked the Golden Jubilee of the founding of the camps. The *Grenada* issue marks the twentieth anniversary of the World Health Organization with dramatic references to heart, kidney, lung and cornea transplants. The four stamps from *Finland* epitomize the services of the Red Cross as governed by the Geneva Convention. Among stamps with designs associated with health and welfare many commemorate specific events, the *Australian* stamp for the fifth World Gynaecology and Obstetrics Congress of 1967 being an example. Others, like the annual Red Cross issue from Finland, deal more broadly with the subject, and usually provide for a donation to charity through a specific charge for each stamp over the postal value.

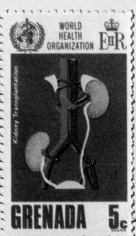

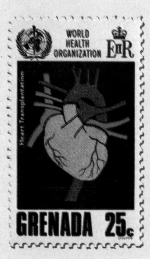

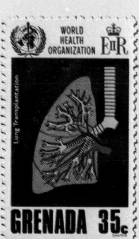

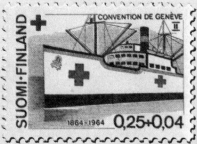

Christmas stamps appear annually from all parts of the Christian world, expressing the Christmas nativity message in different ways; either by direct reproduction of old masters or by special designs as in the case of the *Gibraltar* stamps [far right]. A more secular approach is seen in stamps from *Great Britain* [above] where the designer, Rosalind Dease, deliberately placed the emphasis on children and toys as symbolic of the 'Happy Christmas' referred to on these stamps themselves and the *Botswana* issue of 1970.

Space stamps have caught the imagination of thousands of collectors who assemble large collections of designs which have any association with the theme, however tenuous. A more controlled collection concentrates on stamps issued by the two major space-exploring countries (the *United States* and *Russia*) and stamps like the four-part *Singapore* issue with its earth satellite tracking station which plays a valuable part in ensuring the safety of astronauts. Russia is represented by the double stamp which paid tribute to the twin space flights in 1963 of Vostock 5, piloted by Colonel Valery Bykovsky, and Vostock 6, when history was made by the only woman space pilot, Valentina Tereshkova. To commemorate the first landing on the moon in 1969 the United States had printed in advance a 10¢ stamp which was released as Armstrong stepped on to the Moon. The earlier Apollo 8 mission to survey the moon was marked by the 6¢ stamp inscribed 'In the beginning, God . . .'.

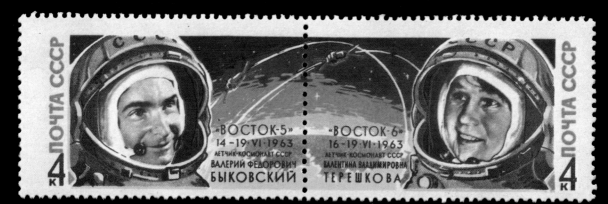

Literary stamps offer scope for collectors whose cultural interests cover philately and literature. *Nicaragua* neatly combined its philatelic commemoration of the 50th anniversary of Interpol with a series of 12 stamps devoted to classic detective stories. The author's name appears on the coloured book spine and the 'plate' page is a portrait of the character he created. The three shown here are Inspector Maigret, Perry Mason and Sherlock Holmes. *Czechoslovakia* has honoured 20th-century cultural personalities in caricature, examples being Ernest Hemingway, George Bernard Shaw and Maxim Gorky. Shakespeare and Dickens anniversaries resulted in international philatelic commemoration. National tributes include *British* stamps for the sesquicentenary of John Keats' death and the bicentenary of Walter Scott's birth and the 8¢ *United States* stamp of 1972 picturing Mark Twain's famous character, Tom Sawyer as painted by Norman Rockwell in 1937.

SUOMI-FINLAND 0,25

3к 1971 БЕЛАЗ·540 ПОЧТА СССР

Australia
QANTAS
FIFTIETH ANNIVERSARY 1970 6c
GEORGE HAMORI RBA

GULF AVIATION FIRST FLIGHT TO LONDON BY VC10 – APRIL 1970
QATAR 1 DIRHAM

DEUTSCHE BUNDESPOST
20
75 Jahre Nord-Ostsee-Kanal 1970
Muster

1812·1962 4c U.S. POSTAGE
LOUISIANA

NEPTUNE RUBY
SINGAPORE 15c

INTERNATIONAL TOURIST FAIR
AERIAL ROPEWAY
7d
GIBRALTAR

3'- MALAWI
DIESEL RAIL CAR

Transport in all its variety – land, sea and air – from all periods is represented worldwide. These examples include travel by hovercraft, canal and aerial ropeway, apart from the more conventional methods. The Mississippi riverboat was a happy way of marking the 150th anniversary of Louisiana's statehood recalling a bygone age when the river was everybody's highway and life revolved around the comings and goings of those grand old paddle boats. The *Australian* strip of three stamps recalls the pioneer flights to Darwin from the south, and the triumph of Ross Smith who blazed the England-Australia trail in 1919 following a careful land survey of the Northern Territory by Lieutenant Fysh in a car as primitive as Ross Smith's aircraft.

3c
New Zealand CLASS "W"

SR N6 Hovercraft
1/3
J. ANDREW RESTALL HARRISON AND SONS LTD

CAPT. WRIGLEY, POINT COOK–DARWIN
5c
ACROSS
AUSTRALIA
ERIC THAKE RBA

CAPT. ROSS SMITH, VICKERS VIMY 1919
5c
G-EAOU G
ENGLAND-AUSTRALIA
ERIC THAKE RBA

NORTHERN AUSTRALIA 5c
LIEUT. HUDSON FYSH SURVEYS
ERIC THAKE RBA

Shapes: The accepted, convenient shape for a stamp is a vertical or horizontal rectangle since this permits simple perforating. The first breakaway was made by *Cape of Good Hope* with is famous triangulars of 1853. In recent years, innovations have included the issue of irregularly shaped stamps such as the *Malaysian* earth satellite station issue meant to represent the conventional idea of broadcasting radio waves. The *Maltese* Christmas stamp of 1968 is shaped with a stable in mind. Unorthodox shapes, like that within a second one assuming the outline of the Rock of *Gibraltar*, are not often used because of the additional production costs. Long narrow stamps are not popular because they are difficult to mount. They are issued occasionally: see the *Western Samoa* stamp and that from *Papua & New Guinea* which splits across the middle to provide two 10¢ stamps.

JAMAICA 6ᵈ    JAMAICA 6ᵈ    JAMAICA 6ᵈ

Sport of all kinds accounts for a very large proportion of commemorative and thematic stamps, issued with unfailing regularity. Every four years the Olympic Games provide the reason for a world-wide flood of Olympic Games issues from the major participating countries and practically every non-participating country, simply because Olympic Games stamps will sell. These issues are normally identifiable by the five rings of the Olympic symbol. Regional events such as the South Pacific Games are commemorated by issues from the countries directly involved and national sporting anniversaries such as the Diamond Jubilee of the *Fiji* Rugby Union account for one-country issues. Some collectors find the whole field of sports stamps too vast to cope with and they concentrate on issues concerned with one sport alone. A slowly developing theme is cricket stamps in which the issues from *Jamaica, Guyana* and *St Lucia* for the MCC West Indian Tour of 1969 feature prominently. The first two were printed in sheets of nine stamps with ornamental margins, shown in part at the top of the page. The most famous of *Great Britain's* sports stamps is the 4d value of the June 1966 issue for the World Football Cup competition overprinted ENGLAND WINNERS and released in August 1966 following England's success.

44

US 6c
XX OLYMPIC SUMMER GAMES · MUNICH 1972

100 MEDINA · CORREO AÉREO · URUGUAY

ИГРЫ XX ОЛИМПИАДЫ 1972
10 K
ПОЧТА СССР

2 CENTS
DIAMOND JUBILEE OF FIJI RUGBY UNION
fiji
FIJI R.U.

XVIII. LETNÍ OLYMPIJSKÉ HRY 1964 TOKIO
2·80 Kčs
ČESKOSLOVENSKO

XVIII. LETNÍ OLYMPIJSKÉ HRY 1964 TOKIO
1·60 Kčs
ČESKOSLOVENSKO

E II R
SAILING WEEK 1972
COOLIDGE AIRPORT
ST. JOHN'S
NELSON'S DOCKYARD
antigua 35c

1970 COMMONWEALTH GAMES
12½c
SWAZILAND

ITALIA
1971 giochi della gioventù
L.20
I.P.S. - ROMA - 1971
A. PERONE

4d ENGLAND WINNERS
World Cup 1966
HARRISON AND SONS LTD

ČESKOSLOVENSKO
1·20 Kčs
TOKIO
XVIII. LETNÍ OLYMPIJSKÉ HRY 1964

ITALIA
1971 giochi della gioventù
L.50
I.P.S. - ROMA - 1971
A. PERONE

1869 - 1969
UNITED STATES 6c
PROFESSIONAL BASEBALL

4th South Pacific Games, Papeete 1971
21c
Papua & New Guinea

80 F

PARC NATIONAL AKAGERA

LIONS

REPUBLIQUE RWANDAISE

1972

JEAN VAN NOTEN

21 c

Chondropython viridis

PAPUA NEW GUINEA

BEAN BLISTER BEETLE 9 d

Mylabris dicincta

MALAWI

25 n

RED LOCUST: DESTROYS OUR CROPS

RED LOCUST
(Nomadacris septemfasciata)

ZAMBIA
CONSERVATION YEAR 1972

SEAHORSE

E II R

1 CENT

TURKS & CAICOS ISLANDS

PRAYING MANTIS

Sphodromantis sp.

3/-

MALAWI

SAMOA I SISIFO

PAINTED CRAB

Carpilius maculatus

4 SENE

URANOTHAUMA CRAWSHAYI

MALAWI 8 t

LUCHTPOST 65 CENT

Heliconius Doris Metharmina

SURINAME

PAPUA & NEW GUINEA 10 c

Hyla iris

7 c

Carettochelys insculpta

PAPUA NEW GUINEA

Natural life in all its forms, from the lordly lion to the shells of the seashore, has provided stamp designs by the thousand. A frequent custom is for an issue to be devoted exclusively to a single facet of nature such as moths or butterflies. Another set from the same country may deal with marine life and a third with insect life. Quite often the scientific name of the creature or insect pictured on a stamp appears without its common name being quoted at all. When collecting natural history stamps it is preferable not to include stamps with animals foreign to the issuing country. This occurs when, for instance, a European zoo releases a publicity set picturing 'foreign' animals and can, in fact, be misleading if young collectors do not realize for instance, that giraffes and lions are not native to Frankfurt-am-Main but merely on show in the local zoo!

2 F

ORNITHACRIS CYANEA IMPERIALIS

REPUBLIQUE RWANDAISE

JEAN VAN NOTEN

15 c

Clanculus puniceus

KENYA

POLYNESIAN STONE DEITY

20c PITCAIRN ISLANDS

PITCAIRN ISLANDS

Baskets 20c

6 CENTS

SINGAPORE

15 CENTS

SINGAPORE

1 CENTS

Pi Pa

SINGAPORE

15

PAPUA & NEW GUINEA

CLAY HEAD FOUND AT LESRA · UGANDA

1'30

KENYA UGANDA TANZANIA

50c

ROCK PAINTINGS · KONDOA · TANZANIA

KENYA UGANDA TANZANIA

1 CENT

Mirudhangam

SINGAPORE

tinashi

nederlandse antillen 15 +5c

BOTSWANA 3c

ROCK PAINTINGS, TSODILO HILLS
TO COMMEMORATE THE OPENING ON 30·9·68
THE NATIONAL MUSEUM & ART GALLERY

6F

INSTRUMENTS DE MUSIQUE AFRICAINS

REPUBLIQUE RWANDAISE

Native cultures: The artifacts of primitive peoples, native dances, musical instruments and ancient rock drawings and carvings have appeared on many stamps. These issues can be arranged to illustrate developing cultures and show how, despite the Western influences, many peoples cling to old superstitions and faithfully perform age-old rites and ceremonies. Many of the curious art forms survive to provide the interested collector with a theme which prompts further reading and study in order to understand fully the significance of the objects on the stamps. The *Pitcairn Islands* provide an ancient Polynesian stone carving and some of the beautiful basketwork carried on today by the descendants of the Bounty mutineers who were marooned on Pitcairn in 1790. Rock paintings from *Botswana* and *Tanzania* suggest a link between two early civilizations.

MAKISHI MASK

POSTAGE

ZAMBIA 15n

# Stamps Used for Propaganda

It is, perhaps, a little difficult to draw the line between commemorative stamps and those used for propaganda purposes. To the purist, a commemorative stamp is one which specifically marks an anniversary of a past historical event, or commemorates a current celebration associated with a particular country. A propaganda stamp does not necessarily commemorate anything but seeks to publicize an idea. How then can a stamp, which commemorates the 25th anniversary of the founding of the United Nations and is issued by a state which did not even exist in 1947 (when the United Nations was established), really be a commemorative issue?

When the first 'independent' United Nations stamps appeared in 1951 they were blatantly propaganda issues. The postal affairs of the United Nations headquarters, sited in New York, were catered for by the United States Postal Administration (now, incidentally, the U.S. Postal Service). Separate United Nations stamps were not necessary, but the propaganda value of having every piece of U.N. mail leaving New York franked with U.N. stamps of international postal validity was a valuable public relations exercise which was self-supporting, since stamps purchased by collectors and mounted into their albums in mint condition paid the costs of designing and printing without the United Nations Postal Administration having to provide any postal service. As various

anniversaries of the many United Nations special agencies have fallen due, the United Nations have issued special stamps and, basically, they are propaganda issues rather than commemoratives.

There are many other issues of individual countries of a purely propaganda nature. Sweden did not 'commemorate' the switch-over from driving on the left to driving on the right but the country did issue a striking stamp to underline the change-over, thus supplementing in a very practical fashion the nation-wide government publicity which preceded the switch. Road safety for children, accident prevention in the home, the prevention of forest fires, the dangers of drug abuse and a wide range of other non-political campaigns in many countries have been featured in stamp designs.

The wider adoption of metrication in weights and measures has resulted in several issues which have been designed to drive the message home, sometimes in a serious vein, as with East Africa, but more lightheartedly by Australia, where four stamps based on a cartoon character must have made Australians take notice of the impending changes.

Straight political propaganda is seldom met with in today's stamps from western-style democracies, but there are many countries who have used them for this purpose. Pre-war Germany provides a good example when, in 1934, as a prelude to the plebiscite on the return of the Saar from French occupation, two stamps appeared, one with two hands holding a lump of coal boldly inscribed 'Saar' – a reference to the rich coal mines of the area, to which Germany laid claim – and the other with the German eagle, again inscribed 'Saar', and the swastika of the rising Nazi party.

Russia has made generous use of stamps for propaganda for purely political ends. It is the custom for 'commemorative' stamps to appear on pretexts which would certainly not result in stamps from other countries. They are, in fact, thinly disguised propaganda issues designed to publicize the achievements of Russia by her people in general and some individuals in particular and to further the overall cause of Communism.

Another form of propaganda, in which Russia has also taken part, is the issue of stamps urging the preservation of wild life and publicizing the concept of conservation. In recent years, the United States has taken part in such campaigns with the issue of stamps printed in blocks of four, each stamp featuring a North American animal which is in danger of extinction through the carelessness of man.

There are many American stamps issued in general support of American ways of life and American institutions, but not related to specific commemorations. The themes have ranged from statements by famous Americans (a total of six stamps issued during 1960–61 and referred to as the 'Credo' issue) to a cheerful design of a clown's head planned merely to remind everybody of the existence of the American circus and the fun it brings into everyday life.

FUR SEAL
UNITED STATES
8¢
•WILDLIFE CONSERVATION•

UNITED STATES
8¢
CARDINAL
•WILDLIFE CONSERVATION•

JOHN MUIR CONSERVATIONIST
5¢ UNITED STATES POSTAGE

•WILDLIFE CONSERVATION•
BROWN PELICAN
8¢
UNITED STATES

•WILDLIFE CONSERVATION•
UNITED STATES
8¢
BIGHORN SHEEP

QATAR
POSTAGE
DIRHAMS 20
TRAFFIC DAY

POLICIA FEDERAL ARGENTINA
SEGURIDAD Y EDUCACION VIAL
20 PESOS
R. ARGENTINA
CASA DE MONEDA    VII-1968    E. MILIAVACA Dib.

STOP
Deutsche Bundespost
30
Neue Regeln im Straßenverkehr
1971

FEUERWEHR
30
DEUTSCHE BUNDESPOST
MUSTER    1970

DEUTSCHE BUNDESPOST
5
NEUE REGELN IM STRASSENVERKEHR
Muster

65
SVERIGE
OLLE KÅKS del.    MAJVOR FRANZÉN sc.

9P
Oak: Quercus robur

Conservation and preservation are the themes of this page of propaganda stamps. Four fast-disappearing forms of American wildlife are given helpful support by the block of *United States* stamps. John Muir, through whose efforts California's great redwood trees were saved from extinction, is shown [top right]. Road safety is publicized on stamps from *Argentine*, *West Germany* (including the international road stop sign), *Sweden* and *Quatar*. Fire fighting from West Germany and tree conservation from *Great Britain* and the Argentine complete the picture.
[Opposite page] A wartime Hitler-head stamp of Germany defaced by a grid used pending the issue of new stamps, which endeavoured to expunge the memory of Hitler and his Nazi Party.

REPUBLICA ARGENTINA
25 c.
SEPTIMO CONGRESO FORESTAL MUNDIAL
CASA DE MONEDA    1972    H. VIOLA DIB.

The conversion to metric weights and measures is tackled in very different ways [above and right] by the East African Post and Telecommunications Department of *Kenya*, *Uganda* and *Tanzania* (note how the three names are variously placed to avoid giving preferential treatment) and by *Australia*. A political drive for prosperity through quality and reliability (the PQR campaign of 1973) was propaganda for industry in *Singapore*. Short-lived *Biafra* reminds the world of Nigerian atrocities, *Gibraltar* adds its contribution to the theme of the enlarged E.E.C. with a stamp incorporating the flags of the nine members of the Community and *Malawi* advertises its switch to decimal currency in place of the old British pounds, shillings and pence.

Prevent drug abuse

United States Postage

**8**c

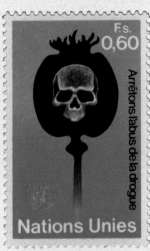

MONACO

LUTTE CONTRE LA DROGUE

JUMELET

0,50

F.s. 0,60

Arrêtons l'abus de la drogue

Nations Unies

HALT! RAUSCHGIFT IST SELBSTMORD

O. STEFFERL 1973

REPUBLIK ÖSTERREICH

**2**S

Four views [above] on the world-wide problem of drug abuse, each design graphically conveying the horror of the subject, epitomized by stamps from the *United States, Monaco*, the *United Nations* and *Austria*. [Left] A literacy campaign issue from the *People's Republic of Southern Yemen* (formerly Aden), and stamps from the *British Virgin Islands* and the *Republic of Maldives* support-ing the work of the United Nations International Children's Emergency Fund. UNICEF, a United Nations agency of great international repute, is concerned not only with health and welfare but with educational projects designed to equip under-privileged children for their future as responsible citizens. [Below and lower left] Five of the stamps issued all over the world to mark the 1968 Human Rights Year organized by the United Nations. *Gibraltar's* reminder that Magna Carta (AD 1215) was an historic 'Human Rights' document is especially interesting. All these stamps include the flame symbol of the Commission for Human Rights which is concerned with legal rights of people everywhere.

35 FILS

يوم العلم العالمي ٣٥

PEOPLE'S REPUBLIC OF SOUTHERN YEMEN

POSTAGE بريد

**International Literacy Day**

BRITISH VIRGIN ISLANDS 30c

EⅡR UNICEF

25th Anniversary of UNICEF

TWENTY FIFTH ANNIVERSARY OF THE UNICEF

UNICEF

**5**L

REPUBLIC of MALDIVES

20 sene

INTERNATIONAL HUMAN RIGHTS YEAR 1968

SAMOA I SISIFO

PAPUA & NEW GUINEA

HUMAN RIGHTS YEAR

**5**c

HUMAN RIGHTS 1968.

MAGNA CARTA

**1**s

GIBRALTAR

FALKLAND ISLANDS

1968

HUMAN RIGHTS YEAR

**2**D

HUMANOS 3'50 PTAS

AÑO INTERNACIONAL DE LOS DERECHOS

19 68

CORREOS

F.N.M.T.

ESPAÑA

20c (U.S.CY.)
TOURISM
E II R
BRITISH VIRGIN ISLANDS

COSTA RICA 90 cts.
CORREO AEREO
.I.C.T.
EMBLEMA "INSTITUTO COSTARRICENSE DE TURISMO"
AÑO DEL TURISMO DE LAS AMERICAS—1972

CORREOS DE CHILE
AÑO DEL TURISMO DE LAS AMERICAS 1972
E° 3.50
CASA DE MONEDA DE CHILE 1972

MONTSERRAT
50c
THE 5TH TEE & FAIRWAY

50
JEDERZEIT SICHERHEIT
Muster
DEUTSCHE BUNDESPOST

WESAK
CEYLON
6 CENTS

WESAK
CEYLON
35 CTS

CRAWFISH INDUSTRY
JASUS TRISTANI
Tristan da Cunha
10d

REPUBLIQUE FRANÇAISE POSTES
C E P T
Ve ANNIVERSAIRE
0.50
EUROPA

europa
1/6
C E P T
MALTA

AEREO
INDUSTRIA PETROQUIMICA
HC CH HC CH
31c.
REPUBLICA ARGENTINA
CASA DE MONEDA    1971    H. VIOLA Dib.

DEUTSCHE BUNDESPOST
oipc interpol ikpo
40
1923–1973
Muster

CELULOSA Y PAPEL
65c.
REPUBLICA ARGENTINA
CASA DE MONEDA    1971    H. VIOLA Dib.

HELVETIA
40
INTERPOL
1923-1973
oipc igpo INTERPOL
JÖRG MAUERHOFER    COURVOISIER S.A.

A mixed bag of propaganda designs ranging from tourism and sport in the West Indies (*British Virgin Islands* – beach holidays and *Montserrat* – golf), *Costa Rica* and *Chile* to a boost for the crawfish industry re-established in tiny *Tristan da Cunha* on the return of the islanders following their enforced evacuation in 1961 owing to a volcanic eruption. Each year most of the countries in the Conférence Européenne des Postes et Télécommunications (CEPT, founded in 1949) issue stamps in a uniform design to emphasise their unity of purpose in seeking improvement and unification of postal service throughout Western Europe. Those shown are from *France* (1961) and *Malta* (1971). Industry in *Argentine* (the refining of petrol and paper-making), the famous Interpol organization linking the information services of police forces throughout the world (*West Germany* and *Switzerland*), accident prevention in the home (*West Germany*) and stamps from *Ceylon* for the Buddhist Wesak Festival complete the page. Each aspect of propaganda covered here can be developed into a multi-national collection of stamps on its own.

LUTTE CONTRE LE RACISME
MUSIQUE
30c
REPUBLIQUE RWANDAISE
O. BONNEVALLE

LOVE
US 8c

AR EGYPT
1972 ١٩٧٢
جمهورية مصر العربية
YOUR HEART IS YOUR HEALTH قلبك هو صحتك
WHO
POSTAGE
20 M
٢٠

EL TELÉGRAFO
ECUADOR conmemora 75° aniversario
del Decano de la Prensa Nacional.
$.1.30
CORREO
AÉREO
N. ORDOÑEZ CH.

SUOMEN LEHDISTÖ FINLANDS PRESS
Kaksisataa vuotta Tvåhundra år
1771–1971 0,50
SUOMI FINLAND

أول دستور ١٩٧١ FIRST CONSTITUTION 1971
٣٥ فلساً 35 FILS
POSTAGE
جمهورية اليمن الديمقراطية الشعبية
PEOPLE'S DEMOCRATIC REPUBLIC OF YEMEN

भारत INDIA
1947 1972
भा.प. P. 20
७५

LIBAN لبنان
٥ ق.ل
كهرباء ELECTRICITE
بريد جوي AVION
5 P

PABLO PICASSO
Nations Unies · École internationale
NATIONS UNIES 1.10 F.S.

ORGANIZATION OF AFRICAN UNITY
RINDERPEST
CAMPAIGN
1'50
TANZANIA UGANDA KENYA

MAURITIUS
peace and progress
United Nations
Silver Jubilee
1945–1970
10c

100 ЛЕТИЕ ПАРИЖСКОЙ КОММУНЫ
VIVE LA COMMUNE
6 КОП
ПОЧТА СССР 1971

GUYANA
SOUTH AMERICA 15c
FAO
25th ANNIVERSARY of UNITED NATIONS

Black and white musicians in harmony
support the U.N. campaign for freedom
from racism – *Ruanda Republic* [top left].
The *United States* stamp is for general use on
letters of goodwill, and the more down-to-
earth heart stamp from *Egypt* ('your heart
is your health'), a bit of World Health
Organization propaganda for the U.N.
Other stamps deal with the history of the
press (*Finland* and *Ecuador*), industry in
*Lebanon* (electricity grid), justice in the
*People's Democratic Republic of the Yemen*
(whose first constitution in 1971 superseded
that of the former kingdom), maintenance
of standards in *India*, the Silver Jubilee of
the U.N. (*Mauritius* and *Guyana*), the International Children's School of the U.N. in
Geneva, the rinderpest campaign of the
Organization of African Unity and a
*Russian* contribution to the centenary of the
Paris Commune of 1871.

# Designing Stamps

Stamp designs do not just happen. Even the simplest of designs has to be planned and often more thought goes into a simple, effective design than one which results in a hotch-potch of detail which is lost in its miniature stamp-size form, and is almost meaningless to anybody who does not bother to find out what it is all about.

Certainly so far as British stamps are concerned, a great deal of thought and careful preparation lies behind every design, even that of the current definitives, with their simple, beautiful and dignified bust of the Queen as the main feature. After a great deal of experiment it was finally decided to dispense with any ornamentation and use only the Queen's head and the indication of value for each denomination. Arnold Machin, the artist finally commissioned to do the work, then modelled the head and shoulders in relief preparatory to its being photographed to provide the basic design of the new stamps. It became necessary to complete three different plaques before Machin satisfied himself that the highlights of the features were exactly right for the production of the delicate bas-relief effect on which the success of the final design depended.

When new issues of commemorative stamps are proposed three artists are usually invited to submit designs based on a Post Office brief which lays down the essential features, such as any necessary inscriptions, but leaves the subject in general as wide open as possible.

The selected artists then research the subject of the proposed issue and frequently find that locating suitable source material is more arduous than the actual designing itself. Conversely, there are occasions when source material is so plentiful that the selection becomes difficult. For instance, when it was decided to include village churches in the series which is gradually dealing with various aspects of British architecture, the problem was: which five out of many thousands of churches could be considered 'typical'? The artist whose ideas were eventually accepted (he was Ronald Maddox) travelled hundreds of miles visiting likely churches and eventually chose five which showed fine examples of Saxon, Norman, Early English and Perpendicular architecture.

The Village Churches issue was exceptional in that all the churches illustrated were in England. Normally, care is taken to ensure that all parts of Great Britain are represented in an issue of this nature. This was evident when in 1966 it was decided to issue 'special', as distinct from 'commemorative', stamps featuring the British landscape, the idea being to promote tourism. The outcome was four somewhat 'modern' scenes from Sussex (for England), Antrim in Northern Ireland, Harlech Castle in Wales and the Cairngorms to represent Scotland.

Similar considerations led to the final selection for the Rural Architecture issue of 1970 where cottage properties typical of the four regions were required. England was the problem stamp because of the country's wealth of regional cottages and the difficult choice eventually fell on a Cotswold limestone dwelling.

At intervals, there have been issues of stamps for 'General Anniversaries'. Their purpose has been to acknowledge anniversaries of varying character each falling within the same year. Such issues face the artists with the problem of three or four designs disparate in their themes but which must, essentially, fall into line as a recognizable set of stamps. British designers have been remarkably successful in achieving satisfactory results in these difficult circumstances and there have been cases where two, and occasionally three, artists have each contributed to such a set but have co-operated to ensure the harmony of design throughout the issue. A very good example is the General Anniversary issue of 1970 in which anniversaries connected with the signing of the Declaration of Arbroath, Florence Nightingale, the International Co-operative Alliance, the Pilgrim Fathers and the Royal Astronomical Society were dealt with successfully by two artists, Marjorie Saynor and Fritz Wegner – a remarkable design achievement.

The very popular 1972 Christmas issue featuring angels was another example of thoughtful designing. The successful artist, Sally Stiff, decided on the angel theme for the stamps and searched among medieval Italian pictures for her models. She then made a collage for each of the designs by using velvet, braid, lace and other materials in the chosen colours and these were then photographed for final reduction to stamp size. This method obviated the need to paint in shadows since they were created by the lighting used during photography and thus preserved the relief effect so noticeable on the finished stamps.

Generally speaking, those responsible for selecting the designs finally used have good reasons for their choice. However, whenever the Post Office puts on displays of designs submitted for an issue but not accepted, there is always argument concerning the merit of the designs that did not quite make the grade. Another feature of these periodic exhibitions is the preparatory art work for the finally accepted designs. Ideas tried out and rejected by the artists and the evolvement of the final choice from a score of 'roughs' all indicate just how much thought and care precedes the work which, in minuscule from, finally faces acceptance or otherwise, by the stamp-buying public, few of whom realize what has gone into the designs they so unthinkingly criticize.

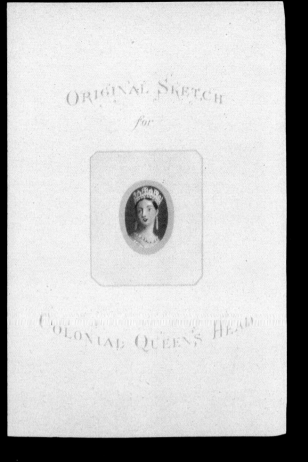

These two delicate watercolours were painted by Edward Corbould to guide the engravers making the dies for early Chalon head stamps of *Van Dieman's Land* (Tasmania) and the Britannia type of *Barbados*. The head is from the 1837 full-length portrait of Queen Victoria by Albert Edward Chalon, R.A. Two British Shakespeare stamps of 1964 are shown together with an unissued essay (preliminary drawing) using the 'Swan of Avon' theme. Below are suggestions by David Gentleman for possible future British issues from 'The Gentleman Album', a collection of essays discussed at a design seminar.

The British stamps of 1970 for the centenary of the death of Charles Dickens posed design problems simply because there was such a wealth of material available. Four different 5d stamps printed joined together and illustrating scenes from Dickens' novels [above] were finally issued. The successful designer was Rosalind Dease who had also submitted a portrait design [far left] and Marley's ghost [above left]. The 50th anniversaries of the first flight from England to Australia and the first crossing of the Atlantic by air were included among the events marked by the General Anniversaries series of 1969. The issued stamps, designed respectively by Philip Sharland (5d) and Michael and Sylvia Goaman (1s 9d) are shown [left] together with unsuccessful designs by Clive Abbott [above and below]. A Goaman design for one of the Concorde stamps is shown [below right].

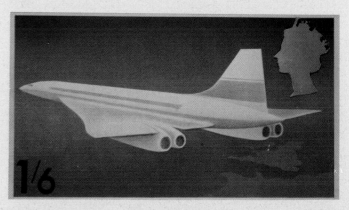

[Right] To encourage British art students to take a serious interest in the specialized work of minuscule design required on stamps, the Post Office and the Design Council, in conjuction with the Royal Society of Arts, annually sponsor student competitions. These four designs were submitted by Kasia Charko, a student at Leicester Polytechnic, and were among the prize-winning entries in a recent contest in which an industrial theme was specified. This student concentrated on industrial archaeology ranging from old artisans' cottages to pithead gear of the early 19th century and the early use of railways for haulage. The yearly bursaries awarded by the Post Office have attracted some very good entries year by year, and the development of those students with a flair for this type of design is carefully studied by the Post Office Stamp Advisory Committee with a view to inviting them to submit possible designs for actual stamps.

Christmas stamps are among the most difficult to design with any real sense of originality. The religious theme of the nativity offers little scope, which is why so many countries opt for straightforward reproductions of work by the old masters and simply employ an artist to design a suitable frame and draw the lettering required. All the British Christmas stamps to date have stressed the nativity with the exception of the 'secular' series of 1968 when Rosalind Dease designed a series of three, using children and toys as the theme [see the 4d stamp illustrated above] and the Wenceslas stamps of 1973 designed by David Gentleman. Arnold Machin, designer of the definitive Queen Elizabeth stamps, submitted preliminary artwork [right] but the idea was not developed further. On another occasion Bradbury Wilkinson & Co. Ltd, noted engravers and stamp printers, proposed two nativity designs [far right and below] based on stained glass windows. Although the idea was not adopted at the time a series of three stamps, designed by Messrs Clark, Clements and Hughes and based on the story of the nativity as shown on stained glass windows in the north choir aisle of Canterbury Cathedral, were accepted in 1971. Special scaffolding was erected in the cathedral to enable the designers to take coloured photographs of the subjects and thus ensure accurate reproductions on the finished stamps.

Artwork on which the United States George Gershwin commemorative issue was based shows the colour 'swatches' indicating how the overlays produce the finished stamp [top right] portraying Gershwin and three characters from 'Porgy and Bess'. The artist selects colours suited to his subject, but it is not always possible to reproduce them without additional printing runs. This accounts for the differences between the artwork and the stamp. The £5 orange stamp of Queen Victoria [right] was the largest stamp ever used in Great Britain. It was adapted from a £5 telegraph stamp by the deletion of the world 'telegraphs' and the insertion of 'postage', the remaining spaces at either end being filled with ornaments. An essay of this £5 (postage) stamp was prepared for inclusion in the King Edward VII series but the stamp was never issued. A printing from the original De La Rue die was sold as a souvenir at the British Philatelic Exhibition in 1971, with a small defacement in the lower right corner to prevent misrepresentation.

Shortly before *France* collapsed in 1940, Winston Churchill offered France complete union with Britain, and a 2fr 50 stamp [above] indicating union by dual portraits of King George VI and President Lebrun, was designed by a French artist, Albert Cheffer. Edmund Dulac adapted this for a proposed 2½d *British* stamp. Dulac's drawing is illustrated [left]. However, when France surrendered on 10 May 1940, the project was abandoned.

58

**5d** Salisbury

**9d** ST. PAULS ✝ LONDON

Subjects covered by Britain's special (as distinct from commemorative) stamps are growing in variety. A set issued in 1969 opened a continuing series on British architecture with some of the country's great cathedrals. From among many designs submitted, the Post Office Stamp Advisory Committee had to select those most likely to appeal to the public, with the result that many original approaches to the theme were finally rejected in favour of what many regarded as miniature picture-postcard views. The imaginative designs shown, of St Paul's and Salisbury Cathedrals, were among those not accepted. In the final choice, Salisbury did not appear but St Paul's found a place on the 9d value of the issued stamps, all designed by Peter Gauld. The interest created by this cathedrals issue (which included St Giles' Cathedral, Edinburgh, and the new Roman Catholic Liverpool Cathedral) encouraged architectural issues on regional cottages, modern university buildings and village churches. Although not architectural in the fullest sense, bridges were the subject of a 1968 issue when the periods covered ranged from the ancient Tarr Steps on Exmoor to the elevated section of the M4 Motorway at its approach to Chiswick flyover.

**9d** ST. PAUL'S CATHEDRAL

3<sup>D</sup> BERMUDA

Christmas 1969

8c
BRITISH SOLOMON ISLANDS

[This page] The Crown Agents, a quasi-governmental organization set up to cater for the commercial and industrial needs of British colonies, still act for the remaining colonies and some independent British Commonwealth countries, in the design and printing of stamps. Artwork commissioned by the Crown Agents and proofs of the finished stamps includes underwater treasure trove from *Bermuda*, an orchid for a *Malawi* stamp and a *British Solomon Islands* Christmas stamp. Artwork of a porcupine was adopted for one of the *Swaziland* definitives of 1969.

[Opposite] This is an example of the careful preparatory work done by David Gentleman for the eight-value 1966 issue commemorating the 900th anniversary of the Battle of Hastings. Using the Bayeux tapestry, Gentleman sketched, in reverse, appropriate scenes and then cut woodblocks. These were 'pulled', in black, to positive and colour values were adjusted. The finished artwork was then reduced to stamp size and, although printed in photogravure, managed to retain the illusion of needlework of the tapestry.

SWAZILAND

1<sup>C</sup>

PORCUPINE

MALAWI 9<sup>d</sup>

Disa ornithantha

Red ground orchid

BERMUDA 4<sup>d</sup>

Christmas 1969

8c
BRITISH SOLOMON ISLANDS

E II R
Surgeon and Officer (Light Company) 20th Foot 1816
8<sup>d</sup>

ST. HELENA

SWAZILAND

1<sup>C</sup>
PORCUPINE

MALAWI 9<sup>d</sup>

Disa ornithantha

Red ground orchid

61

# Something Went Wrong

While a piece of pottery or porcelain, be it a Staffordshire figure or a Sèvres vase, showing a flaw in the making, loses 'face' with the connoisseur, a stamp that is undamaged but has a design flaw fascinates the stamp collector. Depending on the quantity issued before the flaw is corrected, the imperfectly designed stamp is often worth more than the correct version.

Such flaws may be the result of ignorance on the part of the designer or just carelessness. Either way, the collector makes the most of his chances by adding variety to his collection. One example is the portrait stamp of Sir Edward Codrington, issued by Greece in 1927 for the centenary of the Battle of Navarino when, in 1827, the British Admiral commanded a combined British, French and Russian fleet which routed the Turko-Egyptian fleet, then attacking Greece. Designed and printed in Greece, the first printing of the stamp captioned the portrait SIR CODRINGTON. A second printing corrected the error and read SIR EDWARD CODRINGTON.

India provides another example. The first definitive issue following the declaration of independent dominion status featured, quite naturally, aspects of Indian life and culture. The much-used 1 anna stamp portrayed the medieval god Bodhisattva Semhandra Lokesvara, based on a sculpture in the Lucknow Museum. When the stamp appeared the entire image was reversed with the seated Bodhisattva looking to his half right with his left hand resting on his left knee. The engraver of the die from which the printing was prepared forgot that he had to engrave in reverse to print the correct way round. Within a year a revised version of the stamps appeared. Once again both stamps are common and easily available.

One of the most extraordinary mistakes occured on the German Democratic Republic stamps of 1956 commemorating the centenary of the death of Robert Schumann. The fine portrait had as a backdrop a musical score – part of *Schubert's* setting of Goethe's poem 'Wanderers Nachtlied'. Within two days the redfaced officials of the post office withdrew this hybrid stamp and shortly afterwards Schumann appeared again, this time backed up by part of the musical score for one of his own songs 'Mondnacht'.

A literary faux pas on the part of France provides another example when a stamp was issued in 1937 to mark the 350th anniversary of 'Discours de la Methode', a philosophical treatise written by René Descartes, often described as the father of modern philosophy. A representation of the title page accompanied a portrait of Descartes on the stamp but, un-happily, it read 'Discours *sur* la Methode', a design error which the pundits were quick to seize upon. A corrected version of the stamp soon followed, but, oddly, the incorrect stamp is worth only about 20p (50c) in mint condition compared with the 40p ($1) usually asked for the corrected stamp.

The classic howler among stamp designs was perpetrated by the designer of the 1903 issue of the newly formed Crown Colony of St Kitts-Nevis in the West Indies. The association of Christopher Columbus with the Caribbean suggested a picture of the explorer sighting St Kitts in 1492 – through a telescope. Unfortunately, the voyages of Columbus pre-dated the first recorded telescope (that of a Dutch optician, Hans Lippersheim of Middleburg) by over 100 years.

Separate from unintentional errors on the part of the designer there is another class of errors for which the printer must take the blame. Generally, these occur when surcharging a stamp (that is, altering its face value either up or down by printing a new value on the basic stamp), or applying an overprint which may be commemorative in nature, or alters the status of the stamp from a normal definitive to being a postage due or air stamp but does not affect the face value of the stamp itself. The errors are normally those of omission so that a stamp which missed being surcharged or overprinted may be found joined to a properly surcharged one.

In some cases stamps have been specially printed in colours differing from the first printing and then surcharged to provide new values. If a sheet of these stamps misses the surcharging the result is the creation of the basic stamp in a rare officially unissued colour. Two valuable examples are a South Australian 4d printed in blue (valued at £500 – $1,250) instead of purple, the blue being normally surcharged 3-pence, and a 6d St Helena printed in red instead of blue (valued at £750–$11,880), to receive a surcharge reading one penny which was omitted. The normal 6d is blue.

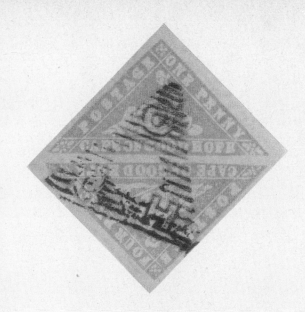

Early and modern errors are represented here. The 4d Western *Australian* of 1854 results from laying down two sets of lithographic transfers to provide the complete design. The swans were laid down first in correct position to take the frames at the second operation, but one frame was laid down inverted and the error was not noticed until after some of the stamps had been printed and sold, thus providing collectors with an error now worth about £2,000 ($5,000). An emergency printing of the *Cape of Good Hope* triangular stamps was made in Cape Town when supplies printed in London went astray. The engraving was crude and collectors nicknamed the printing 'wood-blocks'. A cliché of the 4d value was accidentally transposed to the 1d plate and one of the 1d clichés to the 4d plate, thus producing a red 4d (instead of blue) and a blue 1d (instead of red). Joined pairs of either error are extremely rare, the one

illustrated being worth at least £5,000 ($12,500). The 24¢ *USA* stamp of 1869 is one of three values (15¢, 24¢ and 30¢) of America's first bicoloured set of which an odd sheet went through the press the wrong way up to receive the second colour. As a result, the pictorial inset is inverted in relation to the frame, producing a rarity now worth about £5,000 ($12,500). The first 4d value of the Queen Elizabeth issue for the *Pitcairn Islands* should have pictured the island's school – as the caption indicated. The building shown, however, was the school-teacher's house, and since it was quicker (and cheaper) to alter the ..

caption than the picture, a second printing appeared correctly captioned. *Pakistan* started off on the wrong foot with its first issue after independence in 1948 by pointing the Islamic star and crescent emblem to the right instead of the left; the corrected version appeared the following year.
The errors concerning the *South Australia* 4d blue, the *St Helena* 6d red, the *St Kitts-Nevis* 'Columbus' stamp and the *Indian* 1a stamps with two images of the god Bodhisattva are discussed on the facing page. Errors of design seldom occur because of the careful research by stamp designers, but the errors due to actual printing mishaps are far more usual. An example is a North Borneo stamp of 1897, a sheet of which was first found with an inverted vignette when a large stock of this stamp was purchased by a dealer in 1929.

[Above] One of *Malaŵi's* stamps of February 1973 described the butterfly illustrated on it as *Euphaedra Zaddachi*. In fact it was *Amauris Ansorgei*. A new printing of the stamp with the correct name appeared within a few months. Both are readily obtainable. Errors of this kind are unusual. More common are those where a caption on a stamp is spelt wrongly, an example from North Borneo being 'Jessleton' for 'Jesselton'.

The two *Greek* stamps of 1927, one incorrectly inscribed SIR CODRINGTON and the other corrected to read SIR EDWARD CODRINGTON, referred to on page 62, are illustrated on the far right. They were printed in Greece which might account for the error. The corrected version is worth about *three times* the stamp with the error. A less excusable error was made on a *Jamaican* stamp of 1921 when the Union Jack was wrongly drawn, showing a narrow band of white where there should have been a wide one, and vice versa, in the horizontal stripe at left. A new printing later in the year corrected the error. A check on which is which exists in the watermark. The multiple crown CA (sans serif capitals) occurs on the inaccurate printing and CA (in script capital letters) in the corrected version. The former Belgian colony of *Ruanda Urundi* broke up in 1962 to become the Republic of Ruanda and the kingdom of Burundi, and Ruanda stamps were made by blocking out the old inscription in silver ink and overprinting the new name Republique Rwandaise. The new republic prepared 20fr and 50fr stamps in 1963 for the Freedom from Hunger campaign by overprinting the lower silver bar 'Contre La Faim', but the stamps were never issued; special 'Contre la Faim' stamps were later printed showing the three ears of wheat which symbolized the campaign. The suggestion was made that the republican post office suddenly realized it was scarcely appropriate to have man-eating beasts such as a leopard and a lion and lioness on 'Freedom from Hunger' stamps. The unissued stamps had already been distributed to the philatelic press, and although an attempt was made to recall them, a few are still in private hands and are very rare.

[Right] *East Germany* issued two stamps in 1956 (10pf and 20pf) to mark the centenary of the death of Robert Schumann, with a portrait of the composer against a background score of a Goethe poem set by Franz Schubert! Music lovers pointed out the anomaly and new stamps were brought out with part of the score for Schumann's song, 'Mondnacht' substituted. All four can still be purchased cheaply because the post office released the entire printing of the error to avoid undesirable speculation.

[Left] While scientists are able nowadays to navigate ships by remote control, such sophisticated practices are not known to the *Fijian* natives who prefer to paddle their own canoes. But on the first printing of the King George VI 1½d stamp there was nobody in charge of the canoe! A second printing put this right to the satisfaction of the native mariners. This particular Fijian issue secured fated for the 2d value with a map of the islands was intended to show how the International Date Line (180° longitude) cuts through the islands, so that the traveller can go back a day in time simply by crossing the date line. However, the engraver at first omitted the vital 180°; it was added to the second printing of the 2d value and to a 2½d value added to the series later. A used example of each variety can be purchased very reasonably.

[Above] Printing errors on *American* stamps are very unusual. One of the most extraordinary occurred when the yellow background to the Dag Hammarskjold memorial stamps of 1962 was inverted so that instead of having a white 4¢ and white highlights on the flesh, the number and the face were yellow, and a white gap appeared around the U.N. building. The U.S. Post Office promptly issued millions of the error, so that any collector could own 'this interesting philatelic item', and thereby incurred the wrath of the philatelic world by spoiling the philiatelic value of the original and genuine error! Similar circumstances surrounded the inverted Red Cross overprint which appeared in *Greece* in 1937 [left]: a substantial printing was immediately ordered to keep speculators from profiting unduly from manipulating the small stock of the genuine mistake. In 1937 France tripped up when commemorating the 300th

anniversary of the publication of Descartes' 'Discours de la Méthode' [above]. The title of the philosopher's historic work was shown on the first printing of the stamp as 'Discours *sur* la Méthode', an error that was promptly rectified. Even so it is the corrected stamp which is slightly more valuable than the error, neither being expensive.

# They look Good - but...

There is something fascinating about forgery. It is difficult not to admire the craftsmanship and skill required to copy a complex creation so exactly that it takes an expert to detect the forgery; stamps have enjoyed their fair share of attention from the forger.

There are two major classes of stamp forgeries: philatelic and postal. The first is the limited reproduction of rare obsolete stamps to deceive the collector who wants to fill a blank spot in his album. The second is the reproduction of common stamps in current use to be used on commercial correspondence as a means of reducing postage costs at the expense of the post office in the country concerned. With this latter class can also be included forgeries made during wartime for use on clandestine mail posted in enemy or enemy-occupied territory. Broadly speaking, all postal forgeries are worth a great deal more than the common genuine stamps they simulate. Conversely, with certain exceptions, philatelic forgeries are worth much less than the genuine article. In both cases a ready market exists for their sale, specifically *as forgeries*, to collectors who have a special interest in them for study, to protect themselves against being deceived. It is, of course, an offence to sell forgeries as genuine, but in the United States it is also an offence to sell forgeries as forgeries: it is, indeed, even an offence to possess forgeries knowingly, although recognized authorities such as the Philatelic Foundation in New York are granted dispensation to own reference collections for purposes of comparing them with stamps submitted for opinion as to whether they are genuine or forged.

Apart from complete forgeries, there are genuine stamps which have forged overprints or surcharges applied. More recently, the interest in postal history has encouraged the application of forgeries of rare postmarks to genuine stamps, on or off cover, and these are sometimes very difficult to detect.

The most famous British postal forgery was that of the one-shilling green stamp of 1870, of which many thousands were used illegally without detection in a post office for a short time, but it was not until nearly 30 years later that the deception was revealed. At London's Stock Exchange Post Office, sheets of forged one-shilling stamps were smuggled in and, obviously with the connivance of the counter clerks, used on telegram forms handed in by stockbrokers' clerks. The stamps were cancelled with the office hand-stamp, and after dispatch of the telegram, the forms were filed for a period and then sent as confidential documents for pulping. When a pulping mill was being demolished in 1898, workmen found some sacks of unpulped forms bearing stamps. They tore the stamps from the forms and offered them to a stamp dealer. The dealer realized they could not be genuine because the combinations of check letters in the corners of some of them did not exist in the genuine stamps. Closer examination revealed other printing defects and the fact that the stamps were without the water-mark of the genuine issue. Investigations based on the date of

the postmarks on the forged stamps revealed that the conspirators had probably defrauded the Post Office of £60,000 ($123,000) by not having to account for sales of the forgeries.

A more recent example of an extensive postal forgery occurred in Australia in 1932 when large quantities of the two-penny King George V head type and the two-penny Sydney Bridge commemorative stamp were forged and used to stamp circulars to promote the sale of lottery tickets. One circular, addressed to a philatelist in Adelaide who realized that the stamp was forged, led to the arrest and imprisonment of the gang concerned.

During both World Wars, the Allied governments produced exact imitations of German stamps. These were smuggled into Germany and used on anti-German propaganda delivered by the unsuspecting German post office. During World War II, French stamps issued by the Pétain government were forged by the Allies and used on propaganda mail posted in France.

Philatelic forgery is less exciting but, generally speaking, it is more of a menace to the collector. One of the best known forgers was Jean de Sperati, who operated quite openly in France. He always sold his 'stamps' cheaply as reproductions, and even signed the back in pencil as a guarantee of their being genuine reproductions! Among his customers, however, were dealers who removed the pencilled signatures and sold the stamps at prices consistent with the genuine article. Sperati's reproductions were much more lifelike than are most forgeries, and tended to deceive on sight unless the buyer was familiar with the characteristics of the printing processes used for the genuine stamps. Although recognized for what they are, Sperati forgeries are in great demand by specialist collectors and the sale of a reference collection of his stamps brought more than £6,000 ($15,000) at an auction in Basle, Switzerland, in March 1972.

All this need not frighten the collector. The vast majority of his stamps will be genuine in every respect. Before buying a valuable item, he can consult an expert committee prior to concluding the deal. In Britain the Royal Philatelic Society, London, and the British Philatelic Association have such committees for his protection, and in America he can consult the expert committee of the Philatelic Foundation in New York. Stamps valued at £25 ($62) or more certainly warrant the cost of a committee's certificate.

This selection of forgeries gives a good idea of the ground covered by forgers of stamps. The *Latvian* air stamp (one of a set of three) is a forgery of about 1930, produced on a very large scale for sale as a cheap set to unsuspecting collectors; it is sufficiently crude that comparison with the genuine stamp clearly exposes the forgery. The two *Cape of Good Hope* triangulars are fair copies, but since they not printed from recess (engraved) plates, and lack the watermark of the genuine stamps, they too are easily detected. The *Ionian Islands* (ceded to Greece by Great Britain in 1864) only issued three stamps, of which the used are much rarer than the unused; and the blue (1d) stamp is a genuine one with a forged postmark while the orange $\frac{1}{2}$d stamp is a complete forgery. The two Montevideo (*Uruguay*) stamps were produced at the famous *atelier* of the Swiss forger, François Fournier. The business was bought by L'Union Philatélique de Genève, who marked all the stamps faux or facsimile, and sold reference collections to philatelists. The three early *Brazil* stamps (60 reis, 280 reis and 430 reis) are lithographic imitations of engraved stamps. The *Leeward Islands* 4d stamp is genuine, but the overprint commemorating the Diamond Jubilee of Queen Victoria in 1897 is forged.

It is curious that so few of the early stamp forgers appeared to appreciate that when the genuine stamp was printed from an engraved plate, the detection of forgeries is a matter of ease because all the early forgeries were produced by lithography

and the difference between the two processes was evident to anybody with even an elementary knowledge of printing. It should also be remembered that the vast majority of the forgeries produced before 1880 were not intended to deceive. They were crude reproductions, generally in inaccurate colours and with blatant imitation cancellations (because used stamps were then more in favour than unused), made as space-fillers for the contemporary stamp albums which tended to have printed spaces for all the stamps which had been issued but which were unlikely to come the way of the average collector. The stamps illustrated on this page are among the better forgeries intended for sale as genuine stamps. The principal forgers operated in Germany, Switzerland and, to a lesser extent, in London. In the United States the local post stamps of the carrier companies were forged by a group known as the Boston Gang.

[Right] A corner pair of the lithographed postal forgeries of the 1932 2d Sydney Harbour Bridge commemorative of Australia used to frank circulars offering lottery tickets.

[Left] An anti-Nazi pro-
paganda postcard printed
in Britain during World
War II, and stamped ready
for posting with a good
forgery of the then current
Hitler stamp, also produced
in London. The red
Hindenburg stamp and the
purple Himmler stamp are
also British forgeries used
for propaganda. [Centre
left] A sheet of 12pf + 6pf
and 3pf + 2pf stamps,
which caricature Himmler
and Goebbels.

Examples of postal forgeries. [Top] A letter
posted from Sicily to Marseilles in 1860.
The 20 grana stamp [top left] and 2 grana
[middle] are forgeries, while the other two
are genuine. Naturally, all the postmarks
are genuine for the letter passed through
the post with the forgeries undetected.
These are among the earliest and rarest of
all known postal forgeries. [Centre] The
second of the Australian postal forgeries of
1932, the 2d King George V head type on
the original envelope. Addressed to Adelaide, South Australia, the stamp was
recognized as a forgery; the rubber stamp
return address led, finally, to the arrest of
the forgers. [Bottom] One of the several
postal forgeries of the very common 25c
'Sower' stamp of France used on a letter-
card from Béziers to Valros. Low-value
French stamps could be bought at thousands of small kiosks which made it easy to
sell the forged stamps to an unsuspecting
public who used them in the normal way.

Examples of forgeries by Jean de Sperati. [Top] A selection sent by Sperati from Aix-les-Bains in 1942 to a stamp dealer in Portugal. The packet containing these stamps was stopped in a postal inspection, and Sperati was charged with evading currency regulations by exporting genuine rare stamps without declaring their true value. Sperati proved that they were forgeries that he had made (which could be sold cheaply and legally if he declared them as reproductions) by making several more just like them. The *Hong Kong* 96¢, and *Lagos* 10s stamps were produced on genuine watermarked paper by fading out a more common value and printing the rare high value in its place. [Left] Two very fine *Swiss* forgeries by Sperati, who also faked the postmarks, the sender's rubber stamp, and the name and address in ink, which appears aged by time. The 2s brown stamp of *Great Britain* is the only British stamp ever forged by Sperati. It is on genuine watermarked paper and has a genuine postmark, which remained when a common 3d rose stamp was faded out chemically before the 2s brown was printed. The rare 1fr carmine tête-bêche stamp of France and the 1s Gibraltar were also among the many forgeries made by Sperati, the latter on watermarked paper. His forgeries are dangerous because they are so lifelike at a cursory glance, even though they were produced by lithography. The cancellations, too, are lithographic but all copied photographically from genuine postmarks. The Sperati business was put up for sale in 1953 quite legitimately while the productions were openly described as reproductions; Sperati died in 1957.

Postage Stamps to be affixed in this space.

Postage Stamps to be affixed in this space.

Dated Stamp.

This is a selection from various forgers. When *Heligoland* was ceded by Great Britain to Germany in 1890, the printing plates for the stamps were in Hamburg, and they were acquired by a firm who reprinted the stamps extensively. The pair [top] are reprints to which a forged postmark has been added to suggest that the stamps are genuine originals. The other 'stamps' at the top and left of the page are complete forgeries with lifelike postmarks. (Very often it is the crude, and inaccurate, postmark which is the first clue to the fact that a stamp is forged.) The Stock Exchange forgery is the most famous of all British postal forgeries. The 1s green [right] has the possible lettering of a genuine stamp (SBBS) in the four corners as does the stamp on the left (lettered EEEE) which could also be genuine but both are forgeries. All the postmarks are genuine, as the forgeries were used illicitly by clerks on telegram forms in the Stock Exchange Pose Office. The Pétain stamps issued by the Vichy government during World War II were forged by British Intelligence for use by the 'maquis' in occupied France. On the left is a genuine stamp. The arrows indicate the tiny differences, the most telltale being the infilled 'F' and the omission of the full stop dots after PIEL and SC in the imprint at the bottom left. The idea of using forged stamps on propaganda material being distributed in enemy territory was first used in World War I when excellent forgeries of Bavarian and Austrian stamps were produced by a firm of British printers whose identity became a state secret until philatelic research solved the mystery.

# Acknowledgments

The authors and publishers would like to thank the owners, authorities and trustees of the following collections and museums for their kind permission to reproduce the illustrations in this book:

**Her Majesty the Queen** for gracious permission to illustrate the following items in the royal collection at Buckingham Palace: *Page 4*, Ceylon 8d; *Page 5* Mauritius 2d; Canada 12d; Nova Scotia 1s; Newfoundland 1s; Victoria 2d; Van Diemens Land 2d; New Zealand 2d; New South Wales 1d; Cape of Good Hope 1d; *Page 6* India 4 annas; *Page 7*, Ceylon 8d; *Page 11*, Great Britain Mulready cover and caricature; Mauritius 1d on cover; *Page 17*, Great Britain 2d Tyrian plum on cover; *Page 55*, Chalon Head and Britannia watercolours and Barbados and Van Diemens Land stamps; *Page 63*, Western Australia 4d; Cape of Good Hope 'Woodblock' pair; South Australia 4d and St Helena 6d; *Page 71*, Great Britain, Stock Exchange forgeries.

**The British Post Office and National Postal Museum, London:**
*Page 12*, Nuneaton Prepaid cover; *Page 13*, Mulready cover to Malta; *Page 55*, Great Britain Shakespeare 1s 6d; London Bridge and Stephenson's North Star essays; *Page 56*, Essays by Clive Abbott and Michael Goaman; *Page 57*, all illustrations of essays; *Page 58*, Great Britain £5 Queen Victoria stamp; £5 King Edward VII essay; Anglo-French stamp essays; *Page 59*, Cathedral designs.

The security printers Bradbury, Wilkinson and Co. Ltd, Thomas de La Rue and Co. Ltd and Harrison and Sons Ltd for various stamps and the designers Clive Abbott, Kasia Charko, Rosalind Dease, David Gentleman, Michael Goaman and Arnold Machin.

**United States Postal Service:** *Page 58* Gershwin Artwork (photo: Belmont Faries)

**Syndication International:** *Page 5*, Stamps of Naples, Tuscany and Sicily; *Pages 6 and 7*, all except Latvia, Lithuania, India, Pitcairn Is. and Baden; *Pages 8 and 9*, all except Nepal; *Page 21*, German inflation stamps; *Page 32*, Czechoslovakia 'Guernica' stamp; *Page 48*, Germany, Hitler stamp; *Page 63*, United States 24c inverted centre; *Page 71*, France Pétain forgeries;

**Crown Agents Stamp Bureau:** *Page 54* Malawi stamp; *Page 60*, all illustrations

**Leo Baresch:** *Page 7*, Baden 1kr stamp

**A.N. Donaldson:** *Page 15*, Kuwait airmail cover

**Francis J. Field Ltd:** *Page 17* U.K. Coronation Aerial Post cover

**David Gentleman:** Page 61 all illustrations

**Stanley Gibbons Ltd:** *Page 5*, Great Britain 1d black and 2d blue; jacket-photography;

**H.R. Harmer Ltd:** *Page 66*, Heligoland forgeries; *Page 67*, all illustrations; *Page 71* forgeries of Heligoland, India, Hanover, Zurich, Norway and Spain; *Page 69*, all illustrations.

**Harrisons:** *endpapers*

**Peter Holcombe:** *Page 8*, Nepal stamp

**Eileen J. Loader:** *Page 70*, all the Sperati forgeries

**London Stamp Exchange Ltd:** *Page 12*, U.S. Patriotic cover; *Page 13*, Wells Fargo cover; *Page 14*, U.S. 'Postmaster' cover.

First published 1974 by
Octopus Books Limited
59 Grosvenor Street, London W1

ISBN 0 7064 0345 2

© 1974 Octopus Books Limited

Distributed in USA by
Crescent Books
a division of Crown Publishers Inc.
419 Park Avenue South
New York, N.Y. 10016

Distributed in Australia by
Rigby Limited
30 North Terrace, Kent Town
Adelaide, South Australia 5067

Produced by Mandarin Publishers Limited
14 Westlands Road, Quarry Bay, Hong Kong
Printed in Hong Kong